Prophetic Preaching

THE HOPE *OR* THE CURSE OF THE CHURCH?

EDITED BY
**Ian S. Markham &
Crystal J. Hardin**

CHURCH
PUBLISHING
INCORPORATED

Church Publishing
19 East 34th Street
New York, NY 10016
www.churchpublishing.org

Cover design by Jennifer Kopec, 2Pug Design
Interior design and typesetting by Beth Oberholtzer

Library of Congress Cataloging-in-Publication Data

Names: Markham, Ian S., editor. | Hardin, Crystal J., editor.
Title: Prophetic preaching : the hope or the curse of the church? / edited by
    Ian S. Markham and Crystal J. Hardin.
Identifiers: LCCN 2019046663 (print) | LCCN 2019046664 (ebook) | ISBN
    9781640652200 (paperback) | ISBN 9781640652217 (epub)
Subjects: LCSH: Preaching. | Christianity and politics--Episcopal Church. |
    Prophecy--Christianity.
Classification: LCC BV4235.P7 P765 2020 (print) | LCC BV4235.P7 (ebook) |
    DDC 251--dc23
LC record available at https://lccn.loc.gov/2019046663
LC ebook record available at https://lccn.loc.gov/2019046664

Contents

Introduction

Ian S. Markham and
Crystal J. Hardin

Politics matters. Unlike sport or food or music, our political preferences are often defining. We are "appalled." We are "afraid." We are "passionate." We are "hopeful." Our language reflects the depth of our convictions. We are not neutral. And, what we believe politically is absolutely shaped by what we believe as Christians. The political really matters.

For the clergyperson, there is a weekly opportunity to share our political convictions. It is called the pulpit. Each week, we find ourselves bringing our political selves into the task of preparing to preach. In most churches, the pulpit is "above" the congregation; the preacher addresses the congregation just after the reading of the gospel. It is an awesome opportunity or, perhaps, temptation.

This issue is acute in today's church. Many clergy in the Episcopal Church are advocating and developing a prophetic preaching voice in response to a landscape marked by increasing polarization and politicization. Often, this involves preaching sermons with direct political themes (and calling for others to do the same). While many congregants respond positively to this, others respond quite negatively. The Episcopal Church, it seems, is no more immune to the temptation of polarization than the secular world. Episcopalians in the conservative minority are often very uncomfortable with politically themed sermons, while liberal Episcopalians may demand the political message from the pulpit. Herein is the problem. The preacher occupies a particular political identity that may be in keeping with, or out of step with, some of those in his or her care. What is a preacher to do? This book offers a collection of essays from a range of preachers working within the Episcopal tradition on the role of the preacher in addressing political issues. Contributors work in varied locations (for example:

Houston, Richmond, London, Washington, DC) and embody varied vocational callings (for example: bishop, rector, professor, college chaplain), offering perspectives enhanced by diversity—from age, race, and gender to preaching experience, prior careers, and political leanings. This book has the spectrum. Republicans and Democrats are in this book. Advocates of "political preaching" sit alongside those who think that "political preaching" is a key reason why the Episcopal Church is in trouble.

While this book seeks to promote and even to produce purposeful conversation around the question of preaching politics (and its interrelationship with prophetic preaching as our current age understands it), this cannot be done apart from engagement with a rather more fundamental question: what is the role of the preacher? This book engages that question necessarily, as it reflects on the answers to it in light of our increasingly polarized society.

In March 2019, contributors gathered at Virginia Theological Seminary to reflect on this project and to offer their opinions, as represented by their essays, amongst their colleagues. As each essay was shared, a rich conversation took place, both on small matters of agreement and critique about individual essays, and on larger matters of understanding (and misunderstanding) about what it means to pastor and to preach in today's political climate. This conversation greatly enhanced the essays that follow, in that each contributor had the opportunity to receive feedback on their essay, which many then incorporated into their finished work. This book then is, truly, the sharing of a dialogue— it is a product of civil, prayerful conversation amongst preachers with differing theological and political viewpoints resulting in thoughtful, contextual approaches to the politics of preaching and the preaching of politics.

In chapter 1, "Preaching Politics: Not Yes or No, but How," Crystal Hardin introduces a taxonomy of the preaching model into which Episcopal preachers appear to be ordering themselves in response to the debate around preaching politics. Critiquing this taxonomy, she promotes instead an alternative vision that could be claimed by the preacher: that of faithful, fellow wrestler. Sarah Condon, in chapter 2, addresses "The Dangerous Potential of the Prophetic Pulpit," leveling sharp critique at the self-professed prophetic preacher, while offering keen observations about the effect of such preaching on diminishing Episcopal congregations. Phoebe Roaf, in chapter 3, "Addressing Power," urges preachers to recognize the inherent power that exists in preaching and in the congregations who receive the Episcopal sermon. She offers a thoughtful process for crafting sermons, one that is aware of the prophetic tradition and pays due attention to scripture, prayer, and context. Roaf's chapter stands in the tradition of the prophetic as inherently communal and aimed at structures of sin. In chapter 4, "Remember Jesus: The Purpose of the Pulpit," Russ Levenson sets out a purpose for preaching that aligns with Jesus's prayer in Gethsemane, one that focuses above all on reconciling humans to Christ and to one another. Boldly, Levenson proclaims that "more is needed than a human solution to a spiritual problem." Alex Dyer agrees with this proposition, yet writes from a different perspective altogether. In chapter 5, "Reclaiming the Prophetic Pulpit," he challenges progressive preachers to reclaim the prophetic pulpit, allowing scripture to act as sure foundation for "comforting the afflicted and afflicting the comfortable." In chapter 6, "Preaching the Jesus Movement," Stephanie Spellers speaks to preaching the Jesus Movement, making the claim that authentic, faithful preaching is always prophetic and urging preachers to consider that neither prophetic preaching nor the Jesus Movement are optional for those who wish to serve Jesus and call others into that service. In chapter 7, "The Political Work of the Church: Go for the Underlying Issues," Ian Markham argues that preaching should always be set in an eternal context; preachers would do well to develop a capacity to "read the signs of the time" such that underlying anxieties and dispositions can be addressed by the preacher in a framework eternal. In chapter 8, "Prophetic Preaching as Sacrament: Finding and Using a Political Voice," Ruthanna Hooke similarly calls for a deeper, more nuanced understanding of the times in which we live, suggesting that this reorientation to what lies beneath troubled waters may meet the need for sacramental preaching that "is political without being partisan, truthful as well as loving, and that can reach us in our soul-weary captivity to the powers." In chapter 9, "Getting the Basics Right," Samuel Wells examines the topic at issue from the viewpoint of one standing apart from the United States (he serves in London), but with some familiarity of American society and politics (having previously served in the United States). He offers a rich set of practical guidelines to be considered by preachers when approaching controversial subjects in sermons and highlights that political sermons should be rare and rooted in pastoral necessity. In chapter 10, "What Succeeds in Preaching: The Way of Blessing," Sam Candler suggests that to bless people is the true end of all effective preaching (even, and especially, when that preaching touches controversy). "Practice blessing people," he writes. A good reminder for all preachers in divisive times. Finally, in chapter eleven, Mark Jefferson gets a last word, reflecting on the necessity of "Reimagining Prophetic Preaching," or preaching politics. He inspires preachers to see this cultural moment as a "new opportunity for action."

This is a book aimed at both preacher and hearer. It is the hope of this book's editors that the preachers find within its pages both practical advice for use in sermon preparation and delivery (particularly as it involves controversial subject matter), as well as positions that provoke thought and challenge formerly held beliefs (regardless of one's current position) about what is meant by prophetic preaching and when, if ever, a preacher should touch upon politics in a sermon. We hope that this book assists the hearers of sermons to grasp the dilemma of the preacher and the deep sense of authenticity out of which the preacher is seeking to work. No one preaches a political sermon simply to divide and alienate a congregation. These preachers preach political sermons because they feel that they have no choice. On the other hand, those who choose not to preach political sermons rarely make that decision thoughtlessly. Just because they do not preach on it does not mean that they do not care about.

Everyone knows that the preaching moment is an important one, and preachers in the Episcopal tradition occupy an influential and formational role—not just as to individual church culture and strength, but as to the Episcopal Church writ large, and its vitality moving forward. It is our hope that the dialogue contained in these pages provokes continued conversation around, and consideration of, the importance of being thoughtful, purposeful preachers, for this time and for all time.

A Word about Language

This book questions whether preaching politics has a place (or should have a place) in the Episcopal pulpit. And yet, at the same time, it works through ideas of prophetic preaching—what it meant to be a prophet in scripture and what it means to be a modern-day prophet, particularly as a preacher. Sometimes, these words are used interchangeably: prophetic, political. This is a sign of the times, as many who call for prophetic preaching mean preaching that explicitly touches on matters of politics. This is complicated by the fact that the term politics is used in our present day to invoke partisan politics. Contributors come at these words, and their myriad implications, differently; and, yet, they all share a hesitation about this language, how it is used, and how its use impacts Episcopal preaching. Readers should note this at the outset, as the manner in which contributors speak to the lack of clarity on this language speaks also to their own positions and the process by which they arrived at them and present them within this book.

Finally

When our contributors gathered for our conversation, we knew that we had the spectrum of the Episcopal Church present. We knew that we had "opponents" and "advocates" of political preaching. But, what we did not know is just how much overlap we would find. All were committed to preaching the gospel. All were committed to the serious theological work of seeking to preach out of the tradition and out of the biblical witness. Like many conversations, once one starts talking one discovers that massive differences from afar look much smaller when one is closer in. This is the gift of grace.

Chapter 1

Preaching Politics
Not Yes or No, but How

Crystal J. Hardin

In the days following the shooting at Marjory Stoneman Douglas High School in Parkland, Florida, social media was a whirlwind of prayers, expressions of horror and grief, calls to action, words of grace and words of hate, all crossing political boundaries in ways that might have seemed unexpected. A horror like Parkland is, as it turns out, a horror universal. The emotions triggered by such an event cannot be contained behind our self-constructed divisions. However, it doesn't take long for communal shock to wear thin. What often follows are words and actions that demonstrate polarization, extremism, and intolerance. Perhaps nowhere is this more true than on social media.

Even in the midst of something like Parkland (especially in the midst of it) Sunday comes and a preacher must preach. Contemplating preaching the Sunday after such an event involves traversing an emotional, intellectual, and theological minefield. How does the preacher speak to such an event? How does the preacher deliver Good News in the wake of tragedy? How does the preacher comfort the afflicted and shield the joyous? Or, should the preacher be comforting the afflicted and afflicting the comfortable?[1] Should the preacher speak to such an event at all? What about all the other ills in the world; how does one choose which events to privilege from the pulpit? Are these even the right questions to be asking? And then, as if this weren't enough, the

---

1. Alex Dyer, in chapter 5 of this volume, speaks to the origin of this phrase and suggests his own answer to my question.

voices cry out from Facebook-land, "If you don't hear this preached about on Sunday in your church, you should get up and leave."

"If you don't hear this preached about on Sunday in your church, you should get up and leave" showed up repeatedly on my Facebook feed after Parkland. On some level, it was justified. The preacher should deliver a sermon of relevance, a sermon that speaks the gospel truth to the minds and hearts of those in the pews on any particular Sunday–a sermon that acknowledges the real-life challenges and tragedies people face and appropriately locates them within the larger Christian narrative. And yet, it doesn't take all that much digging to uncover an inconvenient truth that complicates matters significantly. "If you don't hear this preached about on Sunday in your church, you should get up and leave" does not mean that the Parkland shooting should be noted and addressed in Sunday's sermon. No. It doesn't mean that. Instead, it implies that the Parkland shooting should be noted and addressed in Sunday's sermon in accordance with that person's beliefs about what the problem is (or, worse, who the problem is) and *how the problem should be solved.* It is not a call to engage from the pulpit with the world beyond the church doors. It is a call to engage in a very particular way. A way that, all too often, uses scripture to dismiss, denounce, and divide, many times along party lines. It is a call that does not come alone, but walks hand in hand with another: leave the church altogether on the occasion that the preacher fails to deliver what you wish to hear, which, inevitably, will happen.

"If you don't hear this preached about on Sunday in your church, you should get up and leave" speaks the language of a culture resigned to polarization, fearful of nuance, and angry at what cannot be neatly tucked into this camp or that one. Yet, it is driven, in many cases, by a sincere longing for a change, a better way, a new narrative. People's hearts are breaking. Grief, fear, anger, and frustration often lead one to (reasonably) demand answers, action, and an accounting. Thankfully, some still look to the church for remedy. The preacher's task is to listen attentively for such motivations, to be present to the breaking heart, while resisting the temptation to submit to the toxicity of our present context.

In this chapter, I set out three positions that preachers appear to be claiming in response to our present moment: the apolitical, the visible political participant, and the coded political participant. When the preacher claims one of these positions in response to the insistence of a cultural moment, they subjugate the pulpit to that cultural moment. In other words, the preacher's platform—where they will or will not go from the pulpit—is culture-led rather than Spirit-led. I propose another way, an alternative position, that could be claimed by the preacher: faithful fellow wrestler. This position acknowledges that part of the preacher's task is to model graciousness and civility in speaking to complex issues. This position stands aware of the cultural moment while remaining faithful and flexible, privileging discernment over decisiveness, process over position, and authenticity over perceived absolutism.

The Context

As preachers, we operate in an increasingly polarized and charged political context. We can say little about the news cycle without applause for, or an accusation of, preaching politics, and face assumptions about our own political views based on the use of this word or that in a sermon. Even the Christian call to "love thy neighbor" may be reflexively identified as a partisan policy statement, especially if it falls at the end of a newsworthy week. Given this, some tread lightly into controversial matters, if at all. Others step boldly into the pulpit to deliver a "prophetic word," while challenging their fellow preachers to do the same. Yes, "if you don't hear this preached about on Sunday in your church, you should get up and leave" is the rallying cry of some preachers. As Sarah Condon notes in chapter 2 of this volume, "Clergy often shame other clergy into preaching in a 'prophetic voice' with no regard for their context"; it is demonstrative of a troubling situation. It reinforces a fraught and contrived binary preaching model rooted not in authenticity and openness in its struggle to preach Christ, but instead in the demands of a secular society rife with division, whether real or imagined. Preach prophetically or be irrelevant. Preach prophetically or be complicit. Preach prophetically or don't preach at all.

The call to preach prophetically becomes shorthand for a call to preach politics. The word "politics" means simply "affairs of the cities." Certainly, the affairs of the cities are within the purview of a faithful sermon. Yet, rarely does the mind go to such a neutral point when it hears the word politics. Instead, it is partisan politics that one thinks of and partisan politics that the preacher confronts in the call to preach prophetically. Prophecy, it seems, can be politicized also. This type of preaching is called for by some as a necessary response to our present ills and, in some cases, as an antidote to those ills. If preachers would simply name the societal problem—as we see it—and give some instruction on how to fix it, then the world would be better for it. Right? If preachers would take a stand and call out what (and who) is wrong, we would all have more clarity. Wouldn't we? I'm not so sure.

I believe a sermon of this variety is more likely to stir up divisiveness than true repentance. Those who agree with its message may label it prophetic, to be sure, but the same sermon may be labeled troubling, misguided, or even offensive by those who don't. Those who agree with the message may then point to its offense of those who don't as a sign of its prophetic nature. Before too long, people are leaving congregations because of what is preached and others are leaving because of what is not. And so it goes, a pattern and practice conforming to and reinforcing our context of divisiveness and toxicity with troubling implications for the role of the church and the function of the preacher.

The Church

Within a ten-mile radius of my home are more than twenty Episcopal churches. This fact can lend itself to a consumeristic ecclesiology that is detrimental to the Christian life. It certainly makes it easier to choose the church where the congregation mirrors your own political leanings and the preacher "speaks your truth." If you are looking for a church heavily involved in social justice and advocacy, you need not look too far. If you are looking for a church that calls itself "apolitical," you need only go down the block. Of course, things are never so cut and dried, but you get the point. While these conditions may be exacerbated by our proximity to the nation's capital, we are not the only ones who bear this mark of the times. The merits of choice in church-shopping are beyond the scope of this chapter, but, it is worth noting where the call to "get up and leave" falls short of an understanding of church at its fullest and most life-giving. This is particularly true in our current political and social climate, where there seems to be so little space to gather in community as individuals seen, heard, and valued as children of God.

That people exercise a tendency to group with other like-minded people—and that this extends to church—is not surprising or new information.[2] However, its banality should always be challenged by our ecclesiology. Where the church gathers in eucharistic worship it gathers as the promise and hope of the greatest commandments: love God, love people. Rooted in the filial relationship of Son to Father and the trinitarian relationship in which God encounters us, our individual church communities are, at their best, familial. They require acknowledgment of our belongedness to God and, thus, to one another. They insist upon a recognition of our brokenness and intense need for Jesus Christ. Together as church we do the hard work of living the Christian life, which is imperfect and messy. The joy and challenge presented in such a familial bond awakens us to a profound oneness, a shared human condition whose help is always and ultimately in the name of the Lord. In one another we see ourselves, sin and all. In our oneness, we glimpse the kingdom yet to come.

Politically monolithic congregations where everyone holds a similar partisan ideology are troubling because they risk a limited exchange of ideas. It becomes far easier to fall into "us" versus "them" patterns of speech and belief, mimicking the secular landscape rather than claiming one that is distinctly Christian. It may be easy to conclude then that a politically diverse congregation is the goal, a congregation where people come together across party lines to worship. And yet, congregations like these risk placing certain topics off limits altogether in service of their political diversity. One then wonders if all of the benefits of living together in difference are fully realized. Neither the politically monolithic nor politically diverse congregation is inherently bad. Sometimes, they are inescapable. I suspect that, more often than not, they are creations of our own making, creations that we then reinforce and protect in established community norms, both spoken and unspoken. As preachers, we would do well to be aware of these dynamics, as we play a pivotal role in shaping understanding of church, whether we claim the role or abdicate it.

2. Bill Bishop, *The Big Sort: Why the Clustering of Like-Minded America Is Tearing Us Apart* (Boston: Houghton Mifflin, 2008).

The Preacher

The preacher occupies an interesting space when we gather as church, standing at the intersection of holy liturgy and bodily living. We are, after all, a people of blessed ritual that necessarily happens within a particular context because we are a people. Certainly, it is a part of the preacher's task to offer a word that will illumine our everyday concerns with the light of Christ crucified and to model in the craft of preaching the imperfect and messy work of living the Christian life in community with others. In the preaching task, then, is the opportunity to call attention to the reward of gathering as church, while also speaking to the risk of gathering as church—whether the risk for the particular community is the certainty of sameness or a silence in difference. The opportunity is undermined when preaching politics (or not) becomes a false idol upon which to focus and the measure by which we unnecessarily divide ourselves.

The preaching model that confronts today's preacher seems to require a dividing choice upon entry: preaching politics, yes or no? What once may have been an issue considered by individual preachers on a case-by-case basis within the context of their communities has been elevated to a primary position of public debate. With this elevation walks increased anxiety amongst many—preachers and congregants alike. This isn't surprising. It is consistent with a society that demands clarity of position and devalues nuance. The preacher's position on preaching politics has become noteworthy, both more publicly, as in the Facebook anecdote, and closer to home. It is a matter about which hiring committees and congregations often ask and want clear and decisive answers. Do you preach politics? For some, the answer to this is a position on which to be clear about given the demands of hiring committees, congregations, and the climate writ large. It is a necessary evil. For others, the answer is a marker of identity. It is part of the call. I preach the hard stuff. I preach politics. I'm a challenging preacher. I do not preach politics. I preach the gospel. The gospel is political. The gospel is above politics. I find political preaching deeply troubling. And so on, and so forth.

There is then a certain pressure to pledge allegiance to one side or the other, a pledge antithetical to the discerning spirit needed for faithful preaching. "Do you preach politics?" is issued as a decision to be made seemingly without consideration of congregational context, the needs of individual congregants, or the evolving call of the preacher. For those beginning their formal preaching lives in seminary, the pressure is particularly precarious as preaching does not typically occur within a congregational context. Unmoored from such a context, the preacher risks treating sermons as words to be handed down from on high instead of words formed within the beloved community to whom they are offered. From within this beloved community the call may come to preach on politics, but the response should then be offered as part of a relationship steeped in love and mutual respect. Of course, it would be wrong to assume that a more seasoned preacher is unaffected by the debate surrounding preaching politics, or, as some might say, preaching prophetically. Many a seasoned preacher takes a position on behalf of self or on behalf of staff on the issue of preaching politics. This is problematic where the position taken is in response to the pressures of our current context and acts as a non-negotiable hard edge.

The Available Positions

The false dichotomy that confronts the preacher demands a pattern and practice of preaching as a matter of position, which is problematic because it is less an issue of the single sermon and more an issue of what kind of preacher we will choose to be (or, will ultimately be labeled). Preaching politics: yes or no? Think fast. Plant your flag. Don't look back. Under this model, those that answer "no" often deem themselves homiletically apolitical. Those that answer yes must then navigate their context—with varying degrees of success—often deciding between being a visible political participant or what I will term a coded political participant. Let us look at each of these options.

The apolitical preacher has determined on behalf of themselves, and sometimes on behalf of those preachers working for them, that the message from the pulpit must not invoke politically controversial issues. In some cases, it is the congregation who has clearly called for the apolitical pulpit. This close to the nation's capital, I have heard time and again that people are exhausted by politics that occupy so much of their waking lives. Sunday is a reprieve, a time to be with God and to leave politics at the door. A time to know church family as family and not to be reminded of deep-seated political divisions. In other cases, unity as community is seen as more important than preaching that risks division and anger. To this end, the apolitical preacher may avoid the political message, or what may be seen as the political message, from the pulpit, believing it best to focus on commonalities and to not draw attention to differences. This motivation is not to be dismissed without serious, faithful consideration of the needs of individual communities. And, yet, there is also this question: what is the benefit of holding together political diversity as unity when we stay silent about what has the possibility to separate us? However compelling and well-intentioned the rationale, one might argue that the apolitical pulpit is a fraud. To take the apolitical position is in fact to make a political statement. This is the fatal flaw of this position. Further, the apolitical position is a political statement made by the privileged. What is privilege if it is not the ability to choose what most concerns us? It is a privilege to choose not to wade into controversial political issues from the pulpit where controversial political issues involve the lives of those most vulnerable—the very people that Jesus would have us serve. Privilege should never go unacknowledged or unexamined.

The preacher who operates as a visible political participant has determined that the message from the pulpit must address the political necessarily. How often, of course, runs the gamut. With that said, in my experience, those who hold this position tend to engage more often than not with the political message in a manner that makes obvious their own political leanings. To their credit, the visible political participant does not act as if they have no opinion on current day affairs. They stand where they stand with transparency. They often hold a deep conviction that to speak on controversial matters of public debate is the call of the gospel—what it means to follow Jesus. This is a legitimate position to consider and to honor, while appreciating the risks involved in political preaching. Often, the congregation has consented or even called for the political pulpit, just as in the case of the apolitical pulpit. This is more likely in the case of the politically homogenous, left-leaning congregation. The risk here, of course, is that of an echo chamber where the congregation can demand what they hear from the pulpit: "If you don't hear this preached about on Sunday in your church you should get up and leave." There are times, however, where the congregation has neither consented nor called for the political pulpit and is taken by surprise. Much damage has been done to congregations where a preacher takes to the pulpit to preach a controversial political message with little regard for the congregation's ability to hear it. Preachers of this variety sometimes pride themselves on a congregation's negative reaction to such a sermon. Of course, hard sermons must be preached on occasion. I don't mean to suggest that they don't. Preachers should not censor themselves in order to keep a congregation comfortable or happy. That is also damaging. But, to disregard the needs of those who sit in the pews and preach a political sermon at them rather than as one of them is a violation of trust with potentially far-reaching consequences. Perhaps, every now and then, such a sermon truly walks the way of the prophet. More often, it is not prophetic; it is damaging.

The preacher as visible political participant is the style that claims the most conspicuous and vocal position in the Episcopal Church. However, it is by no means the majority. If the leadership of the Episcopal Church leans left in matters of politics, which it does, then it makes sense that the political pulpit is viewed by the church body as more normative than it actually is. It becomes the pulpit that all others are measured against, because it often occupies the space of the sensational and sometimes demanding. It becomes the pulpit to emulate or the pulpit to push back against. It is this pulpit that most troubles those in more conservative congregations, fearful that an agenda is coming that they must protect themselves from. And it is this pulpit that most troubles those who are exhausted by the divisiveness of our common life and want no part in it—those who might otherwise not call for the apolitical pulpit but who do as a last resort, as a measure of self-protection. This results in interview questions with potential clergy like, "You don't preach politics, do you?"[3]

The preacher who operates as a coded political participant is one who preaches politics implicitly, using timing, context, and language to their advantage to speak a particular message to those with ears to hear within the congregation—without inflaming those with divergent

---

3. Ruthanna Hooke, in chapter 8 of this volume, speaks beautifully to the exhaustion that I hint at here, calling it a "soul-weariness."

political views. Preachers who occupy this role do so for any number of reasons. What I am interested in is the preacher who operates in this manner after determining that the congregational context will not allow for explicit political preaching. I suspect this is the situation out of which the majority of coded political participants preach. At first glance, the coded political participant seems like a good compromise, a less offensive way of staying true to one's political self while preaching to a politically diverse congregation. Below the surface, it is a problematic venture that can be disrespectful to the congregation and compromising to the authenticity of the preacher. Preaching should be rooted in care for community, particularly where it involves potentially controversial or challenging issues. Guest preachers are an exception, although even they are not completely unmoored from congregational context, as the invitation to a guest preacher is presumably issued by a person of pastoral presence within the community. The preaching event does not belong to the preacher, nor is it about the preacher. The preacher is but "a channel, a vessel" for Jesus, "the risen Christ."[4] To speak in coded language is to risk what the preaching event could be. It risks adding to the polarization already running rampant in our society, as the preacher occupies the questionable space of dancing with the ones that agree with her, so to speak. A wink and a nod toward one group from the pulpit is a judgment against another group. Those that are in the know, that get the message, feel good about their position on the same "side" as the preacher. Others sit in ignorance while the preacher belies whatever pastoral relationship may exist (or should exist) and risks undermining the familial relationship so vital to Christian community.

Coded political preaching is an easy habit to form, which makes it dangerous. It is often the case that people hear different messages from the same sermon. This phenomenon may be attributed to the Holy Spirit in some cases, or to poor listening skills, wishful thinking, or pure delusion in others. This cannot be helped, and is not the kind of thing I am addressing here. I am talking about the intentional use of coded language to speak to some members of a congregation while

---

4. Fleming Rutledge, *The Bible and the New York Times* (Grand Rapids: William B. Eerdmans, 1998), 6.

avoiding the potential criticism of others. A preacher ascends the pulpit with a political identity, and that political identity may well cause them to ask this question over that one, to focus on one illustration rather than another. Their political identity may be known, causing listeners to assume an intent that does not necessarily exist. This is not coded political preaching as I am describing it. Instead, I speak to the use of words or phrases with the intent that they be understood by part of the congregation but not all as a form of political speech. The preacher should prepare faithfully and welcome active engagement with the sermon once it has been delivered, which is why the preaching of the coded partisan participant is so problematic. It evades full critique and true engagement by the most possible hearers. After all, how can people truly engage when they have been talked around or talked over? How can people truly engage when they have been given the nod and found in the "know" and in the "right"? Everyone suffers where the preacher fails to model the type of openness to dialogue that is so critically lacking in society at large.

The Preacher as Faithful Fellow Wrestler

The preaching models outlined above are symptomatic of the context in which we live. Indeed, they are models conformed to it. They limit the preacher, discouraging authenticity and discernment by erecting barriers borrowed from a polarized and divisive secular society, but they don't limit the preacher without their permission and submission. It is time to break free. The vision of the preacher I am commending is more nuanced, more human, than that framed by the current debate. It is a vision of the preacher as faithful fellow wrestler.[5]

The preacher as person claims a political identity. The fact is that most preachers wrestle with how their political identities should be informed and confronted by their Christian identities. Here, they share common ground with those in the pews. Ignoring this fact from the pulpit does not make it less true; nor does it make it less likely that those sitting in the pews will make an educated guess about the

---

5. A sincere thank you is in order to the Reverend Elizabeth Henry-McKeever for helping me name this vision of the preacher and more generally for her generosity in helping me order my thoughts for this chapter. I am so grateful.

preacher's politics anyway. Ignoring this fact from the pulpit is a point
of privilege; it is a political act. This is the critique of the preacher as
apolitical. On the other hand, some would allow their political identity
to take center stage in the pulpit, speaking to what any good Christian
should do in this political situation or that one. There is no sense of the
struggle, there is only the arrival at a point of "rightness." There is no
recognition that other opinions may have an integrity and coherence
that can be held before God; there is only *this way*. This is the preacher
as visible political participant. Where the preacher cannot allow their
political identity to take center stage in the pulpit, they may choose
instead to employ coded language to reach those in the congregation
who agree with them without angering those who do not. This is the
preacher as coded political participant. Each of these positions is political. The question then is not whether a preacher will or will not preach
politics. The question is: how is the preacher meant to engage faithfully
with difficult, and sometimes controversial issues, in a manner that is
authentic to the preacher and pastorally sensitive to the congregation?

The question focuses on process, which means that the answer will
be different for different preachers. Perhaps it resembles one of the
three options discussed previously. What it will not be is a decision
made as an absolute. While the process of answering this question
requires the faithful work of the individual preacher, I offer three con-
siderations to keep in mind: humility, engagement, and truth.

"But who am I, and what is my people, that we should be able to
offer so willingly after this sort? for all things come of thee, and of
thine own have we given thee" (1 Chron. 29:14, KJV). A preacher
must begin with humility, asking, "But who am I?" Taking this question
seriously not only inoculates the preacher to some degree against the
risk of preaching their word rather than the Word, but it reminds the
preacher of the gift of what is happening. The call to preach the gospel
is worthy of our deepest gratitude and our utmost respect. Too often,
we take it for granted and use it to our own ends. Before we know it,
we begin believing that we are owed that deep gratitude and utmost
respect from the people to whom we preach because of our position as
God's chosen preacher. Lost is the awe and fear before God at being
called to such a task. Lost is the dependence on discernment and faith
in the bringing forth of a sermon. Instead, we say what we want to say

and too often we say it to our own glory. Lost is the next bit, the best bit: "for all things come of thee, and of thine own have we given thee."

Humility works wonders for the ability to engage. Where one is confident of Christ's authority and has an appropriate knowledge of one's own ability to do nothing of import apart from God, it is easier to become the sort of preacher who is attuned to the concerns of the community. A preacher must be truly accessible as a pastoral leader in order for the preaching moment to be inherently dialectic and relational. By truly accessible, I mean that the preacher should be open to critique, attentive in listening, and committed to what On Being's Civil Conversations Project deems "adventurous civility."[6] Where this is cultivated by the preacher in their relationship to the parish, they may then address somewhat controversial issues from the pulpit knowing that the relationship into which they speak will support ongoing dialogue. Of course, it is critical that the preacher be ever attentive to their process of engagement with scripture as they approach the pulpit. Faithful engagement involves risk. The preacher must submit themselves fully to the lectionary. There can be no position held apart or held above for safekeeping. All positions must bear the risk of being changed and shaped in confrontation with the Word. If the scripture does not challenge and perhaps even condemn the preacher, then the preacher should question the depth of their engagement. A preacher should risk ascending the pulpit with a dislocated hip.[7] Sometimes the limp that results is the witness of the pulpit. Faithful engagement also involves openness: openness to the Word and openness to others. Where the preacher finds their sermon accompanied by a finger pointed at others, then the message has likely been missed. Where the preacher finds their sermon ignoring the elephant in the room, saying little to nothing of people's lived experience, the message never had a chance.

---

6. "The adventure of civility for our time can't be a mere matter of politeness or niceness. Adventurous civility honors the difficulty of what we face and the complexity of what it means to be human . . . [it] is about creating new possibilities for living forward while being different and even continuing to hold profound disagreement." "The Grounding Virtues of the On Being Project," On Being, accessed April 2, 2019, https://onbeing.org/civil-conversations-project/the-six-grounding-virtues-of-the-on-being-project.

7. Genesis 32:22–32.

Finally, the Good News. The truth is what must be preached. It is the message of the day and the message eternal. This truth, God's truth, comes with a certainty that allows for openness and calls us to love. This is a distinct kind of truth. Other truths come with a sort of certainty, too. Defensive certainty. Closed. Self-assured. Self-relying. Our truth rests in Jesus, who requests not our defense, only the risk of our love. While God may be on Facebook (nothing is out of God's reach after all), I doubt that "if you don't hear this preached on Sunday" is God's call to the preacher, nor should it be the standard for the congregation. With that said, this Facebook challenge, and others like it, is informative. It expresses a hunger, not for silence or trivialities or self-congratulating condemnation of others or divisiveness, but for truth. We must meet this hunger with preaching that asks us to be more, that models a way out of this divided discourse we find ourselves in, and that claims a truth all-encompassing. Strike that. That allows itself to be claimed by a truth all-encompassing.

Preaching politics is not a yes or a no. To treat it that way is to risk subjugating faith to politics rather than politics to faith. Meeting the call to preach the Word as a broken person in a broken world to broken people requires submission to scripture and complete reliance on a living, speaking, loving God. That is all. Let us then as preachers point to Christ, submitting all truths to the ultimate truth. When we take that seriously, all else falls into its rightful place.

BIBLIOGRAPHY

Bishop, Bill. *The Big Sort: Why the Clustering of Like-Minded America Is Tearing Us Apart.* Boston: Houghton Mifflin, 2008.

On Being. "The Grounding Virtues of the On Being Project." Accessed April 2, 2019. https://onbeing.org/civil-conversations-project/the-six-grounding-virtues-of-the-on-being-project.

Rutledge, Fleming. *The Bible and The New York Times.* Grand Rapids: William B. Eerdmans, 1998.

Chapter 2

The Dangerous Potential of the Prophetic Pulpit

Sarah Condon

A Vision of Prophecy

In the opening scene of the first episode of AMC's *Preacher*, we see a comet come from distant space and head directly for planet Earth. As it descends upon the continent of Africa, we hear a preacher loudly proclaiming to his congregation that they have been promised a prophet. He starts to ominously paraphrase verses from Revelation 19: "And then I saw heaven opened, and behold, a white horse. The one sitting on it is called Faithful and True. He is dressed in a robe dipped in blood and his name is the Word of God." The comet explodes through the rickety village church, slams into his chest, and knocks the preacher over. The congregation erupts into praise. The preacher stands up and in a cosmically huge voice he tells them to "BE QUIET." There is pin-drop silence. And then the preacher declares, "I am the prophet. I am the chosen one." As that last sentence comes out of his mouth, he literally explodes into a bloody mess all over his gathered congregation.[1]

As Nathan said to David, I say to my fellow preachers, "You are that man." This is what happens when we declare ourselves prophets and the pulpit our center stage. Or at least it is what should happen.

If there is one word that I wish the church would reexamine these days it is *prophetic*. We proclaim preachers prophetic. We aim to teach our seminarians how to preach prophetically. Clergy often shame other clergy into preaching in a "prophetic voice" with no regard for

---

1. *Preacher*, "Pilot," AMC, May 22, 2016, directed by Evan Goldberg and Seth Rogen.

their context. It is perhaps most troubling that it is now acceptable to proclaim yourself a prophet in the pulpit. Since I was asked to address the dangers of the prophetic pulpit, I will begin in a rather discouraging place. We have to honestly address the current state of our church and the way that "prophetic preaching" has come to function in our pulpits. Anyone looking at the quality and theology of preaching in the Episcopal Church right now will see a landscape of well-meaning sermons given to sparsely populated pews.

However, I do not despair. I truly love my church and I actually believe that our denomination is poised, perhaps more than any other mainline tradition, to preach the gospel of Jesus Christ for all people. First, we must do the hard work of looking at where the idea of so called prophetic preaching has landed us.

Who Is in the Pews?

We would be foolish not to acknowledge our plummeting church attendance in a conversation about the quality of our preaching. Since the year 2000, average Sunday attendance in the Episcopal Church has fallen by 300,000 people to a staggering low of 556,744. We comfort ourselves with the idea that all church traditions are seeing decline. Would that this were true. More conservative traditions are seeing growth. I would suggest that, while these churches are not growing because they are conservative, their conservatism leads them to preach about Jesus in a way that the Episcopal Church has almost entirely abandoned. People are going to church. They just are not coming to ours.

Our congregations are facing the realities of aging and death. According to 2014 statistics from the Episcopal Church website, 73 percent of Episcopal congregations report that more than half of their members are over the age of fifty, while 27 percent of Episcopal congregations report that more than half of their members are sixty-five or older. Given that there has not been substantial growth in our denomination in the last five years, it seems reasonable to expect that the average age of membership has only slid more towards the direction of elderly, while the overall number of people in our pews has declined. These depressing but factual numbers matter in the conversation around prophetic preaching.

Preaching prophetically to a room full of grey-haired Christians can seem fumblingly humorous. I've struggled to hold in laughter when I've seen a preacher attempt to tell a room whose average age is seventy-five that this will be the year to really take on world hunger. Preaching at the elderly to solve the world's ills is like using a pool float for a cruise ship. You'll get about five feet out to sea before you realize it was a bad idea.

It's not as though the younger among our pews, few and far between as they may be, are able to fulfill the preacher's edict to do more and be better. As a mother of young children, I feel even less equipped to follow the preacher's worldly imperative to *make a difference.* Between the changing of diapers, the combing of hair, and the fixing of breakfast, I feel lucky to make it to church on a Sunday morning. When I do, I walk in with the weight of the world's expectations on my shoulders. I have heard the news and I have read the articles. I know that it feels like the world is coming apart at the seams. Between my personal strife and the global headlines, the last thing I need to hear is something that will make me feel more helpless.

A Pastoral Disaster

I know I am not alone. People are exhausted. The world is broken. Preaching burdens to burdened people is a pastoral disaster. When we cling to the notion of "prophetic preaching," the needs of the people in the pews go unaddressed. Christians in the twilight of their lives are worried about the realities that haunt their hearts. They may wonder why their adult children will not speak to them and if the promises of Jesus will actually be true in their own deaths. Young families are dealing with the modern expectations of marriage and childrearing. Our single people are struggling in their loneliness. The stark realities and pain of divorce go almost entirely un-preached in the Episcopal pulpit. So-called "prophetic preaching" fails to meet the congregation in its own context and accomplishes very little.

At best, all it does is create a kind of homiletic sound loop. It is reasonable to expect that many Episcopalians hear the same stories on National Public Radio and read the same *Washington Post* editorials that tell us all *what we should be caring about.* The preacher can take to the pulpit and feel momentarily good about telling a congregation that they should care about something, and the parishioners can feel momentarily good about hearing it. But does anything really change? What is the marker for success in this style of preaching? Are global problems really being fixed? Or are we adding to division? Is God's righteousness being enacted, or are we merely allowed to feel self-righteously better than "those other people" who do not care like we do? Scripturally speaking, when it comes to this style of preaching in our churches we look less like the Great Commission and more like Paul's admonition to the divided church in Corinth.

This style of prophetic preaching ignores the scriptural mark of personhood from Paul's letter to the Romans: People do the thing they do not want to do. Paul tells us that the law, or the *ought*, produces the opposite of its intent. Therefore, the more the belabored preacher postures as "prophetic" in the pulpit, the more everyone but those already in agreement will dig their heels in and resist. People do not attend church to receive step-by-step homiletics instructions on how to make the world a better place. They attend church because they are the walking dead in grave need of a redemptive word.

Perhaps worse than ignoring scripture, this style of preaching can ignore the people as well. It can lead to the priests growing angry or frustrated with their flock. Instead of looking out on a congregation and seeing them swimming (or better put, drowning) in their own sin, the preacher finds them troublesome. Instead of a preaching theology that communicates empathy and love, this style begins to make the parishioners seem lazy. The end game of any sermon should never be to make people better people. The final word from any sermon must be the unending mercy of Jesus. That this last line makes me sound conservative or evangelical says everything about the present state of the mainline church.

The Zeitgeist is Killing Us
(and Seminaries Are Helping)

Why is the Episcopal zeitgeist encouraging us to preach this way? There is no one answer. We almost certainly pick up on these tendencies in our wider culture, which is very good at publicly shaming people for wrong actions, wrong views, and wrong beliefs. Social media is ground zero for "prophetically" telling people their political beliefs are evil or misplaced. Additionally, our seminaries share some of the responsibility. Most, if not all, of our denominational seminaries are offering classes on how to be a more prophetic preacher or how to find your prophetic voice. None of the instruction has anything to do with actual prophesying. How could it? We cannot teach people to be prophets. Community organizers, sure. Political preachers, definitely. But calling people into prophecy is the business of the Lord.

If we really wanted to teach clergy what it means to be a prophet in the biblical sense, we would send them into a classroom where people drove nails into their hands and they were rebuked, or they were thrown into a pit, or they were forced to wear dirty underwear. Prophets are called and they suffer—that is the well-worn biblical road of prophecy. Of course, while you cannot teach someone to be a prophet, you can teach them to have a grandiose vision of themselves as they step into the pulpit. And unfortunately, teaching future clergy to think of their preaching as "prophetic" does just that.

If I had a dollar for every time a colleague of mine had bemoaned, "Why won't my people just do what I tell them to?" perhaps I could fund a seminary program that encouraged pastoral and empathetic preaching. My own seminary education drove home the idea that our job was to call people to account in the name of fixing the world. The problem is, that does not work. If our seminary education insisted that we can take to the pulpit and do the undoable—make people better—then it is no wonder that our priests cannot sustain a commitment to church work. It should not surprise us that half of all clergy leave the ministry after only five years. I wonder how much of the blame should fall on this disconnect.

The Conditional Theology That Hurts Us

It is imperative to add that the theology of the Episcopal Church is encumbered by a high anthropology, which means that we believe that human beings are capable of anything that they set their minds to. This plays itself out dramatically in the "prophetic pulpit." I am dumbfounded by the part of the church that both advocates for a high anthropology and yet insists that the pulpit is the place where we tell people what to do. If human beings are so capable, why do they need so much instruction?

At its most heavy handed, this style of preaching might as well be called plain old moralism. Telling people that it is their responsibility to save the environment is not any better than dictating sexual mores. Both of these attempts at preaching put moral imperatives in the place of the gospel. The subtext is the same conditional theology that says Jesus will love you if you do this thing correctly.

To truly preach prophetically, we must know the sin and hurt that haunts our people's hearts and respond by preaching Jesus and him crucified. This is incredibly hard work. Preaching directly to our people is a great deal more difficult than preaching the news cycle or preaching to them as a demographic. It requires that we know our people well. It requires that we humble ourselves to the concerns of the congregation. And crucially, this kind of preaching demands that we take the narrative of our sin and Jesus's redemption seriously for our church and for ourselves. It means that we know that God is in charge and that God's plans for us will be made known. It means ultimate trust in God's grace and goodness for us.

Our tradition can get very nervous with the idea of grace. We are concerned that people will take God's forgiveness for granted. We worry that if we do not tell people what they should care about, they will care about all of the wrong things. I would suggest that the message is actually that Jesus cares deeply about them. No matter what.

Preaching Must Be Pastoral

One of the most pastorally useful lessons I learned about preaching in seminary did not happen in the setting of a homiletics classroom. The institution regularly brought in local clergy to preach or offer talks about practical parish ministry. On one such occasion, a rector came to speak to us about doing ministry with a small congregation. She had spent a tremendous amount of her ministry simply being with her congregation in their day to day struggles. She spoke about how it had shaped her preaching.

She said that each week she would sit down after Sunday worship and make a list of all the concerns of people in her church. Her people faced hardships like divorce, addiction, and loneliness. This list sat on her desk all week, staring at her. She cared about their actual struggles, as opposed to what they "should" be struggling with. As she interfaced with parishioners that week, studied the scripture, and prepared to preach, this priest kept her eyes on the prize. She knew her highest calling was to be attentive to the hearts of her people. When she preached, she knew that the pulpit was a place to speak to the weariness of their hearts with mercy and grace.

Preaching is a pastoral act—especially prophetic preaching. What people need to hear is how Jesus came to save them from their own sin, not all of the sin in the elusive "out there" that we are allegedly burdened with fixing. We have an anxious urge to "prophesy" to people about what they should be doing, but that ignores what the biblical prophets came to do. They were sent to address the idolatry of the human heart. They came to call people back into their covenantal relationship with God. Prophets could only do that because they knew the people they were preaching to. So as preaching people, we have to first get to know what the hearts of our flock are carrying.

A Return to Biblical Prophetic Preaching

I want to call for a return to the kind of prophetic preaching that we see in the Bible. Preaching that has deep concern for the people who hear the words. Preaching that reminds people that to turn away from God is to break your own heart. Preaching that worries about the pain of sin that people carry into the church. Preaching that calls people back into a faith in the only person that can save them: the person of Jesus Christ.

It is worth noting that not one of the Hebrew prophets wanted to be a prophetic preacher. It was horrible work; work that all but killed some of them. A comet making a bloody mess of them would not have been too far off from the vision we get of the prophetic life in scripture. Prophetic preaching in the Bible happens because God compels the prophets to speak. It is not glorious or celebrated preaching, and one certainly should never choose it for oneself.

Moses murdered an Egyptian and then left his cushy palace existence so that he could wander with and prophecy to his people for forty years before dying within view of the Promised Land. His version of the prophetic life was enduring decades of hardship before dropping dead on the cusp of relief. Tradition calls Jeremiah the "weeping prophet" because the whole of his ministry appears to be a torrent of pain. People hated what God told him to say, and they hated him for saying it. While the Lord saved Jeremiah from one murderous plot intended to take his life, God showed him very little compassion. When Jeremiah complained about the difficulty of his calling, the Lord told him that it would only get worse.

The New Testament prophets were far from donning flowing robes and standing in gilded pulpits. John the Baptist is a case study in eccentricity. He was an unbathed man in the wilderness who shouted at people about the coming messiah. Personal hygiene and peculiarity aside, we should not forget that John met his end with his head on the royal family's silver platter. Paul hardly saw a better fate. After a frightening conversion that involved three-day blindness, Paul went on to direct and encourage the earliest Christian communities, but this was no circuit-riding bucolic vision of the country parson. Paul's experience in ministry was colored by suffering, persecution, and jail time. In short, the vision of prophet that we get in scripture does not track with the version of the prophetic preacher that is so lauded in the church. Given our biblical forebears, we might be suspicious of any "prophetic preaching" that gets too much applause.

In this alleged vein of prophetic preaching that our denomination encourages, preachers are not speaking about God and they are not calling people into repentance. Worse still, there is little regard for kerygmatic proclamation wherein the preacher begins and ends in the finished work of Jesus Christ. What we call "prophetic preaching" is so often shorthand for political preaching. Perhaps the most damning part of this approach to the pulpit is that it seeks to correct the listeners rather than to engage them, to chastise instead of empathize, to damn instead of to call towards repentance. They can get the same endless barrage of imperatives from social media. People have stopped coming to church because they are tired of hearing it. I worry that these "prophetic" words are falling on deaf, or nonexistent, ears.

When We Preach Jesus as Prophet

We must take a closer look at how we choose to posit Jesus as prophet. While we might describe Jesus as a prophet, we generally use passages where we can claim he is speaking about modern politics to prove our point. In this equation, the Sermon on the Mount is not about mercy for the brokenhearted, but a dividing line between the haves and the have-nots (as defined by the preacher), and is used to shame people into action. If only such a homiletic tactic actually worked.

Jesus is a prophet in the Hebrew sense of the description, which is to say, he spoke about the future and he called people to reorient their hearts to God. The woman at the well first called him a prophet when he explained her own secrets to her. He recalled his own prophetic presence when he said, "When you have lifted up the Son of Man, then you will realize that I am he, and that I do nothing on my own, but I speak these things as the Father instructed me" (John 8:28). The prophecy of Jesus has everything to do with God placing him there and Jesus knowing people's hearts. If this were the kind of prophetic preaching the church was attempting to do, we might not be looking at so many Episcopal churches closing.

When we talk about the love of Jesus, which is a sacred topic in the Episcopal Church, we often tell only half of the story. We miss what the Lutheran theologian Nadia Bolz-Weber calls, "the blessed exchange."[2] We fail to acknowledge that Christ Jesus sacrificed himself on our behalf. We ignore the depth of the problem of human sin and our profound need to be saved, which can make the church inhabit the same massive denial that the rest of the world espouses. We live in a culture that both adores self-help books and is in the middle of an opioid epidemic. We need to speak a word over people that Jesus came to be their mediator, that Jesus truly placed his arms on the hard wood of the cross so that all might be saved. This is a radically pastoral way to preach. Some might even dare to call it prophetic.

None of this is to say that we are without modern-day prophets. It is simply to suggest that they are not the entirety of the graduating class of any given Episcopal seminary. One need only to look to Martin Luther King Jr., Dietrich Bonhoeffer, or Dorothy Day, who were people who spoke prophetically to the broken community of the world. Like the biblical prophets of old, they spoke to the faithlessness of people's hearts. Of course, they share a common thread: they preached and they suffered, even to the point of death.

---

2. Nadia Bolz-Weber, *Accidental Saints: Finding God in All the Wrong People* (New York: Convergent Books, 2015), 18.

In a world rife with violence and oppression, I cannot help but sympathize with the urge to take to the pulpit with words that touch explicitly on the political machinations of the day. Yet, I know that these words will only be heard by those who are already on my side. Scripture tells me that Jesus, who loved the widows and the tax collectors alike, is calling me solely to preach about him. When I have been tempted to take to the pulpit and righteously tell a congregation about what they should be thinking and what they should be doing, I am often reminded of the words of an important prophet in the Episcopal Church's own history.

A Sinner and a Saint (and a Prophet)

Jonathan Myrick Daniels was an Episcopal seminarian during the civil rights movement. He is often cited for his martyrdom on August 20, 1965, when he stood in front of a young movement worker named Ruby Sales and took a shotgun blast that was intended for her. For years I have heard about this single act of bravery. While it is powerful to preach about such an incredible offering of one's self, it is not often replicated. However, there is an important story from Jonathan's work in a protest in which he embodies everything that prophetic preaching could be.

> After a week-long, rain-soaked vigil, we still stood face to face with the Selma police. I stood, for a change, in the front rank, ankle-deep in an enormous puddle. To my immediate right were high school students, for the most part, and further to the right were a swarm of clergymen. My end of the line surged forward at one point, led by a militant Episcopal priest whose temper (as usual) was at combustion-point. Thus I found myself only inches from a young policeman. The air crackled with tension and open hostility. Emma Jean, a sophomore in the Negro high school, called my name from behind. I reached back for her hand to bring her up to the front rank, but she did not see. Again she asked me to come back. My determination had become infectiously savage, and I insisted that she come forward—I would not retreat! Again I reached for her hand and pulled her forward. The young policeman spoke: "You're dragging her

through the puddle. You ought to be ashamed for treating a girl like that." Flushing—I had forgotten the puddle—I snarled something at him about whose-fault-it-really-was, that managed to be both defensive and self-righteous. We matched baleful glances and then both looked away.

Daniels's account sounds familiar to the current rhetoric of our denomination. Protests are the daily bread of many clergy who see themselves as prophetic. We long to find ourselves on the side of the righteous and we have an almost anxious energy to place ourselves on the right side of the issue. The problem that we encounter as clergy is that the vitriol of a protest can draw lines between humanity and we can find ourselves squared off against a fellow child of God, someone who is beloved to Jesus even if they are not at all beloved to us. Daniels has his own moment of reckoning. His honesty about what he was feeling and the way that he handled it is perhaps the best example of how we can live and preach into the calling of the gospel.

And then came a moment of shattering internal quiet, in which I felt shame, indeed, and a kind of reluctant love for the young policeman. I apologized to Emma Jean. And then it occurred to me to apologize to *him* and to thank him. Though he looked away in contempt—I was not altogether sure I blamed him—I had received a blessing I would not forget. Before long the kids were singing, "I love —." One of my friends asked [the young policeman] for his name. His name was Charlie. When we sang for him, he blushed and then smiled in a truly sacramental mixture of embarrassment and pleasure and shyness. Soon the young policeman looked relaxed, we all lit cigarettes (in a couple of instances, from a common match) and small groups of kids and policemen clustered to joke or talk cautiously about the situation. It was thus a shock later to look across the rank at the clergymen and their opposites, who glared across a still unbroken "Wall" in what appeared to be silent hatred.[3]

3. "Jonathan Myrick Daniels, Seminarian," *Biographical Sketches of Memorable Christians of the Past,* The Society of Archbishop Justus, accessed April 2, 2019, http://justus.anglican.org/resources/bio/228.html.

This kind of "reluctant love" lives at the potential heart of prophetic preaching. By the grace of God, Daniels was able to name his own self-righteousness. He was able to recognize his need to categorize who deserved God's grace and mercy versus who did not. Jesus was able to break through Daniels's internal dialog. And Daniels was able to sing love back to the man whom he had initially believed he was there to correct.

It is not surprising that Daniels was murdered. His heart for people, even those on the other side of his cause, was not hidden. He longed to know and to suffer with people. This is the difficult but necessary work for any preacher of the gospel, but especially for those who are called to be prophetic. It requires the preacher to sometimes sacrifice their own personal feelings about politics or opinions in order that all of God's people would be called into love and forgiveness. It requires not just naming sin, but naming our personal sins. This kind of prophetic word does not insist that other people have a checklist of perfection. This kind of preaching believes that the unearned grace of God is meant for all people. And it trusts that God will use a prophetic word on people's hearts.

Of course, our tendency in the Episcopal Church is not to trust God. We want to be in charge of what the prophetic word sounds like. We have forgotten that God is in charge of where the kingdom of heaven exists. Our rhetoric of the prophetic implies that it's up to us to make the world come out right, as though God is not an active agent in the world apart from us. When we take on the self-decisive mantle of political preaching, we often find ourselves backed into an ideological corner. Like Daniels, we may find ourselves staring at our perceived enemy only to find ourselves loving them, too. My prayer is that we would be humble enough to recognize the prophetic movement of God in that moment.

The Prophets Are Not Always in the Pulpits

When my husband interviewed for his job to lead a church in Houston, we had no idea that God was already speaking a prophetic word over the congregation. Two years prior, in a period when the church had no rector, some of the women of the parish decided that God was calling them into something new. Houston is a diverse city, both ethnically and economically. These white women decided they needed to hear the stories and the needs of people who lived in less white, less affluent neighborhoods. They genuinely felt like God had put a calling on their hearts. No one had stood in a pulpit and told them what to do. Without a didactic sermon in sight, God welled up in the hearts of these women and they were faithful.

They realized that food scarcity was a major issue in the area and they begin a program to provide food for hungry children on the weekends. When my husband accepted the position as rector, the program was providing food for fifty children every week. That seemed like such incredible work. Fifty families every weekend had more food security. Fifty children did not have to go to bed hungry. But God had something bigger planned. In the span of a mere five years that same program now feeds thirteen hundred children. The story is its own prophetic sermon, and we did not even need a pulpit to tell it.

To name Jesus as Lord, Jesus as the only one who could possibly save us from sin, is the most prophetic way we can preach. It is also the most dangerous, at least from an earthly perspective. It means that it is God's plan and not ours that is enacted. It means that we will not be able to make sense of all of the suffering in the world, much less be able to fix it. And it means trusting that God will. It means that the pulpit is not a place where we tell people what to do. Instead, it is a place where we tell people what God has done; then we get out of the way so that we can see what the Lord will do with such a prophetic word.

The Gospel Proclaimed from the Episcopal Church

Despite all of the depressing numbers about our denominational Sunday attendance, and despite the profound lack of enough clergy to work in our churches, I believe God is calling the Episcopal Church into being a church for all people. I believe that a prophetic possibility has been given to our denomination. God has troubled the waters in a way that only God can, and I pray that we would have the hearts to listen.

We are a church that turns no one away. Sexuality, ethnicity, and even politics cannot and should not stand in the way of a hurting world and the doors of your local Episcopal Church. Imagine what it would look like if our prophetic preaching meant a return to the biblical vision. Imagine knowing the hearts of our people and calling them back into relationship with the Forgiver. Imagine what it would look like if church was not one more place with one more to-do list, but instead was a place where people heard over and over again that the Doer of All has done the work.

As dangerous as our current political and prophetic preaching style may be, this kind of biblical prophetic preaching is much more dangerous. It trusts what the letter of John tells us, "In this love, not that we have loved God but that he loved us and sent his Son to be the atoning sacrifice for our sins" (1 John 4:10). Imagine a pulpit where the starting point for any sermon was that we love because Jesus first loved us. In a world full of suffering, sin, and a shaming need to prove our self-worth, a word of grace and mercy preached to all within arm's reach of Jesus would be prophetic indeed.

BIBLIOGRAPHY

Bolz-Weber, Nadia. *Accidental Saints: Finding God in All the Wrong People.* New York: Convergent Books, 2015.

The Society of Archbishop Justus. "Jonathan Myrick Daniels, Seminarian." *Biographical Sketches of Memorable Christians of the Past.* Accessed April 2, 2019. http://justus.anglican.org/resources/bio/228.html.

Chapter 3

Addressing Power

Phoebe Roaf

In our current context, a time of deep divisions within our nation and our congregations, preachers must decide whether and how their sermons should address those in positions of authority. There are many factors a preacher must weigh in making their decision. In this chapter, I set forth a process for crafting sermons whereby the preacher discerns the appropriate message to share with their listeners. While I do not believe that preachers can ignore their local contexts, the objective of preaching is not for the preacher to rant at his congregation in anger or frustration. Rather, preachers are called to enter the pulpit following a period of prayer, discernment and consultation.

Preaching is inherently personal. Miles's Law, which states that where you stand depends upon where you sit, is certainly true for those who preach. My particular perspective is that of an African American woman who came of age in the segregated South. The institution of slavery existed during a time in our nation's history when a much higher percentage of the population was Christian and actively engaged in the church. Unfortunately, many white Americans simultaneously professed their faith in Jesus Christ and turned a blind eye to the atrocities of slavery and the system of Jim Crow that replaced it. Unlike chapter 2, where Sarah Condon focuses on individual sinfulness, this chapter will explore the corporate nature of sin, a topic I was led to by my personal experiences. In particular, passages of scripture where the prophets addressed entire groups of people resonate with me.

God Commissions Prophets

The Hebrew scriptures contain the accounts of the prophets.[1] God commissioned prophets to call the people of Israel back to fidelity to the Lord. Prophets instructed those who had strayed from the faith to adhere to the covenants God had established with them. As you might imagine, it was challenging work. Few groups want to hear the difficult message that they have fallen short of God's expectations.

There were several reasons for the Israelites' collective wandering from God. Sometimes, it was the stubbornness of the people that caused them to depart from God's teachings. When this was the case, God commanded the prophets to address the Israelites. In other instances, the people were led astray by their political and religious leaders. God then instructed the prophets to speak directly to those responsible for fracturing the relationship between God and God's people.

God compelled the prophets to address those in power when the authorities were not abiding by God's priorities of justice, righteousness, and mercy. It is important to note that the prophets were often unwilling participants in God's plans. They neither requested nor relished their assignment. However, because the prophets were convinced that God instructed them to undertake this difficult mission, most of them ultimately heeded God's call.

Two examples illustrate God's directive to the prophets to speak truth to power. First, we consider the story of the prophet Moses, who was tending his father-in-law's flocks when the sight of a bush that was burning but was not consumed caught his attention. When Moses stopped to observe this unusual sight, the voice of the Lord called him by name and commanded him to remove his sandals because he was standing on holy ground (Exod. 3:1–5).

God ordered Moses to instruct Pharaoh to release the Israelites from captivity. Moses was not enthusiastic about the prospect of delivering this message to Pharaoh, perhaps fearing Pharaoh's response. Moses protested to God, providing several reasons why he was ill equipped for the job. However, God was not interested in any of Moses's argu-

---

1. I am post-critical and believe these scriptures as they are written. My argument does not engage a historical-critical analysis of the Hebrew scriptures.

ments. In fact, the Lord became angry with Moses because of his excuses. As far as God was concerned, Moses was the right person for the job. God instructed Moses to speak directly to Pharaoh, the highest political authority in Egypt.

In the case of Samuel, God called a prophet to address religious leadership. Samuel's story began when he was a boy serving the priest Eli. He heard a voice saying "Samuel, Samuel" after he went to bed. Samuel assumed that Eli called him, so he went to see Eli. Eli perceived that the Lord had come to Samuel and Eli instructed the boy on the appropriate response if the Lord returned. The Lord did return. God told Samuel that Eli's house would endure eternal punishment because Eli turned a blind eye when his sons sinned against God (1 Sam. 3:11–14).

The next morning, Samuel was afraid to convey what the Lord predicted for Eli's house. After all, Samuel was only a boy and Eli occupied a prominent position within the Hebrew religious establishment. However, Eli convinced Samuel to share the prophesy.

The stories of Moses and Samuel demonstrate instances where God instructed individuals to convey difficult messages to political and religious authorities. The first thing I note about Moses and Samuel is their reluctance to speak truth to power. They were mindful of the implications involved and entered this work with some trepidation. As I contemplate whether to address religious or political authorities in my sermons, part of the process involves assessing my internal comfort level. Am I excited about the prospect of being able to say "I told you so" to persons who may never have the opportunity to respond? Do I have a smug sense of self-righteousness as I enter the pulpit? Or, am I feeling the weight of delivering a difficult message? Do I question whether this is the correct approach to take? If I do not have a sense of the gravity of the situation, the time may not be right to deliver the message.

Episcopal Preachers Almost Always Address Power

While most of us would identify Pharaoh and Eli as persons of power and influence, we rarely consider ourselves in a similar light. I believe that every Episcopal congregation includes people who wield significant power within their local communities. As a group, we are extremely well educated and often control considerable resources.

Episcopalians hold prominent positions in corporations, non-profit organizations, and governmental entities. We sit on local and national boards and volunteer with many community organizations. Those are all formal positions of authority. Episcopalians also wield informal authority in our homes and schools, exerting influence on family members and classmates as well as work colleagues. Although we don't always acknowledge it, Episcopalians have voice and vote at many tables where decisions that will have a significant impact on the community are being made.

Therefore, Episcopal preachers are almost always addressing those in power. Our parishioners can be encouraged to consider the ways in which they exercise power and to be intentional about the use of their power based upon the promises made in our baptismal covenant. We can do this whenever the lectionary presents Jesus or the prophets addressing those in power, and it doesn't have to be tied to a local or national crisis.

I invite parishioners to place themselves in the position of the leaders being addressed by the prophets or Jesus. For example, when Jesus criticized the scribes and Pharisees for being hypocrites, to what extent are the policies we advocate beneficial to us and harmful to others? During the protracted government shutdown in January of 2019, I asked whether members of Congress and the president would have allowed the shutdown to last for weeks if they had been denied their salaries and health insurance during that time frame? Are we imposing hardships on others that we aren't willing to take on ourselves? Can we empathize with individuals who are impacted by our decisions? Although the institutions we are a part of may not be Christian in orientation or outlook, how do our contributions to important discussions within these institutions reflect our Christian values? Do we seek and serve Christ in all people, loving our neighbors as ourselves? Do we strive for justice and peace among all people and respect the dignity of every human being?

Discerning the Call of God Today

The prophets reluctantly carried out God's wishes because they were confident that they heard the voice of the Lord. For current-day preachers, things aren't always so clear cut. How do we know that our internal nudging has been prompted by God? What if our ego or our personal beliefs are the primary motivation behind our message? Based upon the experiences of Moses and Samuel, we should be attuned to God calling us by our name. God identifies the one God seeks to serve as God's messenger by name. Moses and Samuel may not have immediately known who it was who called them, but both men heard themselves being addressed in a personal fashion.

God speaks to each of us individually, yet there is a role for others to play in the discernment process. In Samuel's case, he relied upon an older, trusted mentor to help him discern God's voice. Those of us called to prophetic ministry can also utilize the discernment of the community as part of our process. Perhaps clergy colleagues can serve as sounding boards. If you are the only clergyperson serving your congregation, other local clergy, seminary classmates, or a spiritual director can provide guidance. As Episcopalians, we acknowledge the importance of collective discernment. Sharing our ideas with others as we prepare to deliver a message that challenges authorities may be an invaluable step in identifying God's voice.

Prayer is also an indispensable component of sermon preparation where the preacher will address powerful political or religious leaders. We become familiar with the Lord's voice when we consistently spend time with God. In our prayers, we learn how God chooses to communicate with us. We can be confident that the Lord is speaking to us when this is confirmed by prayer. On the other hand, preachers who craft sermons apart from a regular prayer routine do so at their own peril.

The Holistic Approach of Jesus

God instructed the Hebrew prophets to speak truth to religious and political authorities. What about God's call to Jesus? Was Jesus commissioned to a similar task during the course of his earthly ministry? Faithful Christians have different perspectives on the question of whether Jesus engaged in activities that may be characterized as political. Some believe that Jesus was immune from the political factions of his day. After all, Jesus did not want to be acknowledged as a king or as God in some New Testament passages. Some Christians characterize Jesus's mission as exclusively spiritual in nature.

My reading of the New Testament suggests that Jesus adopted a holistic approach to his ministry. Jesus spent very little time in synagogues or the temple in Jerusalem according to what is recorded in the Bible. He encountered many people at work, at market, or at meals. Jesus focused as much attention on their secular needs as their spiritual needs. His actions were not limited to assisting people in their faithfulness to religious rules and regulations.

Jesus healed people of their physical and psychological ailments. These miraculous healings may have contributed to the large crowds that followed him throughout the Judean countryside. In addition to curing people of their physical and psychological aliments, Jesus also raised the dead and fed the multitudes. Throughout the Gospels, Jesus demonstrated compassion for those he encountered. He was concerned about the spiritual health of people but his concerns did not stop with spiritual matters. Perhaps Jesus realized that it is difficult to focus on spiritual issues when there are pressing issues in other parts of people's lives. Since Jesus paid attention to practical issues, I believe we are called to serve others in a similar fashion. There are instances when the church can directly provide assistance in the form of food banks and emergency financial assistance. However, what about addressing the authorities who contribute to the conditions that lead others to suffer?

We have examples of Jesus criticizing religious authorities, typically when they engaged in actions that benefitted themselves and hurt others. Jesus overturned the tables of the money changers in the temple. He confronted the scribes and the Pharisees, characterizing them as hypocrites for placing impossible burdens on others. In addition, Jesus addressed political leaders when he was not pleased with their actions. For example, Jesus called Herod a fox (Luke 13:31–35) and he confronted Pontius Pilate following his arrest (John 18:28–38).

From these passages, it is clear that Jesus was not reticent about addressing power. He assisted individuals in need and he reminded political and religious authorities of their responsibility to conduct their duties in a manner that did not demean the powerless. This represents a holistic approach to ministry. Jesus was not confrontational by nature, but he also did not avoid confrontation when he believed it was necessary.

Preparing to Preach

As preachers consider incorporating Jesus's holistic approach to ministry, are there ways to engage in this work without dividing our congregations? When I am preparing to deliver a message that questions those in authority, one step that I take is to confirm that I have correct information about the situation I intend to address. In an age of alternative facts and segregated media sources, it is easy to receive only one perspective of a complex issue. It is worthwhile to spend the necessary time reviewing several sources of information before drawing a conclusion. The last thing preachers want to do is to have parishioners disregard the message because it includes factual inaccuracies. Getting the facts straight is crucial in addressing power.

I also pose questions to my listeners during my sermons. Rather than beginning a sermon by criticizing a particular policy or individual, I ask the congregation to consider whether a certain event is in keeping with their understanding of what it means to be a Christian. How might faithful Christians approach the issue of homelessness in our community? Or third trimester abortions? How are Christians called to respond to our neighbors without health insurance? What level of support is appropriate for the United States to provide to the State of Israel?

Questions such as these invite persons to make the connection between what they believe and what they read in the daily newspaper or hear on the nightly news. Preachers are charged with the responsibility of encouraging parishioners to view their faith as a lens through which all of life is lived, not just an exercise one engages in for two hours on Sunday mornings. This inquiry also reminds us that people of deep faith hold a variety of opinions on these issues. The question is not always whether Christians should have a unified perspective on an issue. A more important question is, does our status as disciples of Jesus Christ influence the issues we should be actively engaged with? In other words, if Jesus was involved in alleviating the suffering of marginalized people in first-century Jerusalem, is this an essential aspect of what it means to be a twenty-first-century American?

Perhaps all of this is an issue of semantics. For some people, posing these types of questions crosses the line into the political realm. However, I do not believe I am engaging in politics when I raise these questions from the pulpit. Instead, I am part of a long line of people called by God to enter the public square to address those in authority.

Jesus's concern for those marginalized by society seems to have been influenced by his mother. Mary anticipated the scope of her son's ministry before Jesus was born. In the Magnificat, the beautiful hymn Mary shared with her elderly cousin, Elizabeth, when both women were pregnant, Mary proclaimed that God would bring down the powerful from their thrones and lift up the lowly (Luke 1:46–56). She acknowledged the Lord's capacity to work through those without power or prestige, as demonstrated by God's invitation to her to serve as the *Theotokos*, the Christ-bearer. In this hymn, Mary describes a God who is intimately concerned with all aspects of our human existence, the sacred as well as the profane. Surely this understanding influenced Mary's approach to raising Jesus.

We hear echoes of the Magnificat in Jesus's first sermon as recorded in the Gospel of Luke. Jesus delivered this sermon following his baptism in the Jordan River and a forty-day period of temptation in the wilderness. When Jesus entered the synagogue in Nazareth on the sabbath and unrolled the scroll of the prophet Isaiah, he read these words:

> *The Spirit of the Lord is upon me, because he has anointed me to bring good news to the poor. He has sent me to proclaim release to the captives and recovery of sight to the blind, to let the oppressed go free, to proclaim the year of the Lord's favor.*
>
> *Luke 4:18–19*

Then Jesus sat down and declared that this scripture had been fulfilled in the presence of those gathered.

Jesus commended the actions of the widow of Zarephath in Sidon during a severe famine and Naaman the Syrian leper. All of this proved to be too much for his listeners. First, Jesus had the audacity to publicly state that his ministry was in fulfillment of the ancient Hebrew prophets, and then Jesus used two people who were not part of his religious or ethnic tribe as examples of virtuous living. People responded to this sermon by attempting to throw Jesus off of a cliff. However, they were unsuccessful.

The fact that Luke's Gospel introduces Jesus's ministry in this fashion has been an important part of my vocational discernment. When I observe those who are oppressed and those who are blind, what is my response? What does God expect of me in these situations? I believe that we serve as God's hands and feet, God's eyes and ears in the world. I am compelled, therefore, to ask other faithful followers how they live into the commission we received at baptism. It's not a political exercise—rather, it goes to the very heart of what it means to be a disciple.

Earlier, I recommended spending time in prayer and communal discernment prior to confronting political and religious leaders. This suggests that sermons addressing power will be proactive rather than reactive. And yet, all preachers will find themselves in situations where there isn't sufficient time for such a deliberative process. By definition, crises and disasters are inconvenient. Significant events on Friday or Saturday may demand that preachers rewrite their prepared Sunday remarks.

In my experience, preachers are the primary theologians in parishes. We assist parishioners in applying the Bible to the headlines on the nightly news or in the local newspapers. Faithful people seek guidance in making decisions that are pleasing to God. Without an explicit connection between biblical teachings and contemporary issues, it can seem as though our faith is confined to Sunday mornings with little relevance for the remainder of the week.

I adopt the same approach regardless of whether the issue happened last week or last year: I pray; I touch base with clergy colleagues; I confirm the facts; and I ask questions. I lived in New Orleans for thirteen years, so I was compelled to discuss the impact of Hurricane Katrina in my sermons in 2005. To remain silent when my flock was struggling with where God was in the midst of such a tragic situation was unconscionable. Asking how God might be calling us to respond to challenging situations is difficult work. Without minimizing the complexity of a particular situation, do the actions of the authorities seem to mitigate or exacerbate the suffering of impacted persons?

One of the questions I asked after the horrendous conditions in the New Orleans Superdome and convention center were revealed following Hurricane Katrina was: how can the United States effectively mobilize to provide humanitarian relief to persons halfway across the world but be unable to provide this relief to her own citizens? I reminded parishioners who questioned why everyone didn't vacate the city after the mandatory evacuation that these very questions came from a position of power and affluence. Not everyone in New Orleans owned a car. Not everyone in New Orleans had a credit card to cover transportation out of the city or hotel accommodations. One of the jobs of a preacher is to create a safe space where their listeners can consider how they might have responded to a particular situation without assets at their disposal.

Addressing power often means speaking directly to the people in the pews, not only elected and appointed leaders. It involves asking questions more than judging and criticizing. Addressing power also includes inviting parishioners to think creatively about new solutions to intractable problems, and to remind listeners that people of deep faith may disagree on the response to these issues. While we may all agree that homelessness is a serious problem, there are multiple ways to alleviate that issue. We don't have to agree on the methods to reach the desired outcome.

Asking questions during my sermons is a way of beginning a conversation with my parishioners. One of the hallmarks of the Anglican tradition is communal discernment. We are called to grapple with significant issues together. There is much to be gained when several people are generating ideas and solutions. And we know that where two or three are gathered, God is in the midst of them, so this is also holy work. There are times when our congregations seek to be comforted and affirmed. In a world where the pace of change is astronomical, the church is often a safe place in the midst of much uncertainty. And yet, as preachers we are also called to comfort the afflicted and afflict the comfortable.[2]

What is clear is that God has called people to this work for centuries. The Lord has commissioned individuals to address religious and political regimes for as long as humans have recorded their interactions with God. Our task is to prayerfully enter into this work with a spirit of humility and trepidation, knowing that no one possesses all of the answers this side of the grave.

---

2. In chapter 5, Alex Dyer comments on the origins of the phrase "comfort the afflicted and afflict the comfortable."

Chapter 4

Remember Jesus
The Purpose of the Pulpit

Russell Levenson Jr.

For I decided to know nothing among you except Jesus Christ, and him crucified.

1 Cor. 2:2

Louisa May Alcott, in her serialized book *An Old Fashioned Girl*, offers a poignant reflection on the value of a soaked-through Christian life: "I don't want a religion that I put away with my Sunday clothes, and don't take out till the day comes around again: I want something to see and feel and live day by day."[1] Her point speaks, at least in part, to the question this chapter will consider: what is the purpose of the Christian pulpit?

There is no question that the Hebrew scriptures and the New Testament offer the preacher a breadth of material about building an internal infrastructure to live moral, ethical, and loving lives. Jesus was, and remains, the greatest of history's preachers and teachers. Jesus's preaching and teaching came not only with his life, but through his words, culminating in salvific death and resurrection and entrusted to his apostles in the Great Commission: "All authority in heaven and on earth has been given to me. Therefore go and make disciples of all nations, baptizing them in the name of the Father and of the Son and of the Holy Spirit, and teaching them to obey everything I have commanded you" (Matt. 28:18b–20a NIV). But when it came to preaching,

---

1. Louisa May Alcott, *An Old Fashioned Girl* (Boston: Little Brown, 1911), 200–01.

what form does the Great Commission take? What did Jesus most hope for those who would receive the mission of the apostles? In Jesus's prayer in Gethsemane we find our answer:

> *My prayer is not for them alone. I pray also for those who will believe in me through their message, that all of them may be one, Father, just as you are in me and I am in you. May they also be in us so that the world may believe that you have sent me. I have given them the glory that you gave me, that they may be one as we are one: I in them and you in me. May they be brought to complete unity to let the world know that you sent me, and have loved them even as you have loved me.*
>
> John 17:20–23 NIV

There are obviously many reasons one climbs into a pulpit, but if we are to take to heart Jesus's prayer on the night before his passion, clearly a primary, if not the primary, motive was to bring about belief in Jesus as Lord and Savior, to reconcile humans to God and humans to one another, and to unify hearts to the Almighty and hearts to one another. This alone, Jesus seems to say, will reveal the deep truth of who Jesus is in order to let all creation know that they are loved.

Working Against the Grain

The purpose of this collection of essays is to take into consideration the value, or lack thereof, of using the pulpit for the purposes of "preaching politics." For clarity's sake, to consider such a question one must be willing to admit if there is value, then such value exists not only for one political extreme but for both, and perhaps for all positions along the political spectrum.

I have had nearly thirty years of experience as an ordained priest, and much of my ministry has been spent preparing for, and delivering, sermons. I have come to believe that one can easily use the pulpit to bring people closer to God or to drive them further away, to draw people toward one another or up and against one another. I know how easy it is to use the pulpit to bring about division and to heal division.

Let us say, for instance, that I have a very firm belief that abortion in every case should be illegal and I use the pulpit to speak on that topic. I make use of scriptures that could back up my position; I find sources from ancient tradition and modern ethical teachings that can support my proclamation; and I end with a rousing appeal to only support political candidates and judges who will take such a firm pro-life position. Let's also assume the same could be done toward supporting a pro-choice position in all circumstances. What would such a sermon do? It would—unquestionably—throw a sword of division in the middle of the congregation.

I am not suggesting for a moment that the pulpit should never be used to take an ethical or moral position. Clearly English evangelicals were the driving force behind the abolition of slavery in the United Kingdom, giving birth to a movement that spanned the globe. At the same time, failing to respond to the rising tide of fascism and anti-Semitism in Nazi Germany during the 1930s is a sin the church will have to live with for the rest of its history.

There is no question that the pulpit and the lectern must be tools to speak toward a more Christian society, but a steady and consistent diet that only speaks or responds to the political winds of interest rubs completely against the grain of Jesus's prayer in Gethsemane, for to speak only of political matters does not get to the root of our cultural divides or the division that may live within our hearts—division that keeps God at arm's length and humans from one another. It may be possible to have an upright and moral life in every way and still miss the point of the good news of the gospel. A preacher's motive in speaking to political issues (consider for instance global warming, gender identity, economic inequality, racism and so on) may, in fact, be noble. It may even be justified in many occasions. But, if it is devoid of a deeper call to follow Christ, it is anemic at best and fails to effect lasting change at worst. It responds only to the issue of the day, as Alcott's Polly suggests, and does not bring about a faith that serves one day to day, minute by minute.

An Example from the Life of John Wesley

We all know the legacy of Anglican clergyman John Wesley, whose preaching brought untold numbers to faith in Christ. But many do not know that for years, even as a baptized Christian and ordained clergyman, he struggled with finding an authentic faith that bound him to Jesus. For a season, he thought he had found a way to respond to that struggle within his soul. He and his brother Charles, along with several of their mutual friends, formed a religious society in 1720 called "The Holy Club." Its members seemed admirable in every conceivable way. They were orthodox in their faith. They attested not only to the Apostle's Creed, the Nicene Creed, and the Athanasian Creed, but to the Thirty-Nine Articles of the Church of England. They lived what, from the outside, appeared to be impeccable lives. They met together several evenings each week, studied pietistic literature, and tried to perfect their daily schedule so that every minute of every day had an appointed duty. They then began to visit and minister to local prisoners. They founded a school in an impoverished area, paying a teacher and clothing local children out of their own pockets. They attended Holy Communion every week, fasted on Wednesdays and Fridays, kept the canonical hours of prayer, and observed Saturday and Sunday as "Sabbath" days to rest, reflect, and pray.

Yet, in spite of this extraordinary combination of philanthropy and piety, John Wesley later reckoned that he was not a Christian at all. Writing to his mother Susanna, he confessed that, while the practice of this form of faith may have been that of a slave, it was not the faith of a son. Religion to him meant bondage, not freedom. In 1735, John Wesley set sail for Georgia to serve as a chaplain to the colonists and a missionary to Native Americans. Two years later, deeply disillusioned, he returned to England. On the journey home, he wrote this in his personal journal: "I went to America, to convert the Indians; but O! who shall convert me? . . . but what have I learned myself in the mean time? Why, (what I the least of all suspected) that I who went to America to convert others, was never myself converted to God."[2] Wesley was doing "all the right things." He was living a moral and upright life, carrying out works not only of piety, but also of social justice and concern for his fellow human beings. But it was not enough. He needed more–he wanted something more. What happened?

_____

2. *The Works of the Rev. John Wesley, A.M.,* vol. 3, entries for 24th and 29th of January, 1738 (New York: Carlton & Porter, 1856), 54, 56.

About six months after writing these desperate words, he attended a Moravian Church service, and there was a reflection on Luther's Commentary on Romans. It was not until this moment, when for the first time he heard–really heard–the words from Paul's letter to the Romans, "The one who is righteous will live by faith" (1:17), that something shifted. All his attempts at righteousness failed to bring him solace; his moral and upright life had left him wanting something more. What he heard when all seemed lost was that righteousness was not about getting it right–it was not even about doing the right thing. He, and the Holy Club, had given that a try, and it just made him feel more miserable. What he heard was that, along with salvation and peace, righteousness was a gift: not something to be achieved, but something to be received.

The Modern Conundrum

Thinking, praying, earnest Christians of our day know that racism is wrong, sexual abuse and harassment are wrong, bigotry against others because of their sexual orientation is wrong, and disregard for the poor and disenfranchised is wrong. There is no question that Christians have an outright obligation to respond to these cultural sins–often only made worse by a lack of political will. But too often, clergy spend too much time pointing out the wound without going deeper and addressing the infection.

The "Black Lives Matter" and "#MeToo" movements are important. They have, in fact, lifted up societal ills that need to be addressed. One will often see clergy at rallies and protests organized by movements such as these. But the modern conundrum is that without a gospel-centered motive of transforming hearts and lives, the problems will only continue. They may subside for a season, but will reemerge in other ways. Many political leaders touted the Black Lives Matter movement as the death of racism. Popular cultural icons told their audiences that the #MeToo movement would finally mean the end of sexual harassment and misconduct. But, if we are honest, neither of those visions are true. No political movement nor cultural trend, as noble as it might be, will bring about transformed lives. The only way to effectively change cultural ills is to change the heart. Only Jesus can do that.

A Lesson for Preachers in the Face of our Political Divides

One of the most divisive issues of our time is racial discord. We cannot deny that. The fact that human beings created in the image of God are negatively, sometimes violently, going against one another because of the color of their skin is simply ungodly—it breaks God's heart. Our culture is looking for all kinds of ways to push back against it. Some take a knee or engage in other forms of protest. Some dig more deeply into their own personal identity, which leads some black people to believe the answer is to be more black and some white people to believe the answer is to be more white. Taking down flags or removing statues seems to only stoke the fires of division all the more. What is a Christian to do?

We received a glimpse into the real answer in the fall of 2017. On October 19, self-proclaimed white nationalist Richard Spencer delivered a hate-filled speech on the campus of the University of Florida in Gainesville. University officials were afraid that the event could turn violent. The Monday before the gathering, Governor Rick Scott declared a state of emergency for the area. The university president, Kent Fuchs, denounced Spencer's white supremacy platform as abhorrent in a letter to students, but said the school could not stop him from renting a student center to give his speech. And so it went. While people won't remember the speech that day, I hope they remember what happened next for a long time. It is a story that should have been on the cover of every newspaper the next morning.

Aaron Alex Courtney, a thirty-one-year-old African American high school football coach, woke up that morning and headed to join the crowd of protestors ready to clash with Spencer and those who came to support him. When the speech was over, a Nazi identified as Randy Furniss, wearing a white t-shirt covered with swastikas, made his way through the crowd as protestors yelled at him, punched him, and spat on him. He seemed unfazed. Courtney had been protesting against Spencer for four hours, when he and Furniss actually came face to face in the crowd. He said, "I could have hit him, I could have hurt him," but something inside him refused the violent opportunity; something utterly transformed that moment. Rather than throw a punch, he had the courage to come up, wrap his arms around that hate-filled man, and say, "Why don't you like me, dog?" He stepped back, then said, "Why do you hate me? What is it about me? Is it my skin color? My history? My dreadlocks?"

Furniss looked away and did not answer. Courtney hugged him a second time, then he said he quit beating around the bush. He pleaded with him. He said he almost broke out in tears and began to get angry because he did not understand this kind of hate. That's when he heard something inside of him say, "You know what? He just needs love. Maybe he never met an African American like this." So he told Furniss to hug him back. And Courtney reached closer—a third time—and that is when Furniss wrapped his arms around Courtney. Courtney asked one more time, "Why do you hate me?" Furniss whispered, "I don't know." At that moment, Courtney, the son of a bishop in the church, heard God whisper in his ear, "You changed his life." A moment later, away from the crowd, the two of them posed for a photograph together. Courtney said, "I honestly feel that was a step in the right direction, for him to take a picture with a guy that he hated when he woke up this morning."[3]

What transformed this moment? Aaron Alex Courtney did something that no one else in the crowd was willing to do: he laid down his own anger, put politics aside, and even laid down his own identity. Suddenly, in that embrace of black and white, everything became gray. But, gray is hard, because it means we have to depend more on the grace and discernment of God rather than our own fixed position.

My guess is that the picture they took together might not have gotten many "likes" from those who followed them on social media. My hunch is God looked down on that moment and said, "I like that." In moments like that the love of God is all that matters. Aaron knew what was needed in that moment. He knew the need of God for that moment. And he reached out in love and did what only the love of God can do.

There is a real lesson for preachers here. The local congregation is a

---

3. Jessica Chia, "Protester hugs Nazi outside Richard Spencer talk, asks 'Why do you hate me?'," *New York Daily News*, October 20, 2017, https://www.nydailynews.com/news/national/protester-hugged-nazi-pleads-hate-article-1.3575977.

petri dish for division over issues. Issues divide, Jesus unites. The goal of the preacher should be to do all they can to respond to Jesus's prayer and promote reconciliation with God and unity among God's children.

In recent years, mainline traditions have seen their numbers plummet. During the last three decades of this extraordinary decline, parish newsletters, topics for adult Christian education forums, and sermons have reflected a consistent pattern. When a church (or its pulpit) makes political issues the primary foci, there comes a time when the parish either works to remove the preacher, or congregants, exhausted by the same kinds of discussions they hear or read on the news outlets, simply walk away.

Such was the case in a parish where I had a number of friends. The priest, out of a deep, personal conviction, got very involved in the pro-life movement. He participated in pro-life marches, made public appearances before the news cameras, wrote articles, and preached sermons on the necessity that Christians be pro-life. This continued for years and, for a long time, parish membership grew as people with pro-life positions chose to attend a church where such a message was consistently preached from the pulpit. All was well and good, until one Easter Sunday, arguably the highest and holiest day of the church year. The sermon included references about the resurrection of Jesus, but it also included a diatribe on being pro-life. The parish had enough. They were hungering for something more than the moral divides around pro-life and pro-choice issues; membership began to decline, eventually the pastor moved on, and the parish fell on hard times. It has since returned to health, in the absence of the former mission to preach first and foremost a call to join and support the pro-life movement.

A Caveat on Pastors and Prophets

I realize a worthy criticism of my position here is that there comes a time when preachers must speak openly, boldly, and courageously against cultural sins and political corruption. The Bible is full of examples. The world needs modern day Jeremiahs; Dietrich Bonhoeffer, Martin Luther King Jr., and Desmond Tutu would easily be identified as modern-day prophets. But prophets are rare. Prophets are given a specific voice for a specific time, and they are empowered to carry out their work by the Holy Spirit. The answer to Paul's rhetorical question, "Are all prophets?" (1 Cor. 12:29), is, of course, "No."

My proposition, however, is not "never," but "not mostly." Thus, before I move to what the pulpit offers preachers that the political arena does not, I need to provide myself an out of sorts. I have, in fact, as a pastor spoken directly from the pulpit to issues of race, gender inequality, sexual misconduct, gender discrimination, and gun violence. I have also spoken out against ungodly political leadership. Why then, you may ask, am I pushing back against using the pulpit as a political tool?

My answer is not that we never use it for such purposes, just that we do not mostly use it in that way. As the case I placed before you here suggests, more is needed than political fixes; more is needed than a human solution to spiritual problems. This is where Jesus comes in and where the gospel of salvation for our souls takes center stage. With that caveat, on we go.

Speaking to the Ache of the Human Heart

What is the deep and primary purpose of the pulpit? Let us circle back to that encounter between Randy Furniss and Aaron Alex Courtney. Moved to embrace a man who hated him, and then moved to ask him "Why do you hate me?" Courtney received an honest confession: "I don't know." It was the beginning point of healing the sin of hatred that kept both men at arm's length.

Most theologians would call Courtney's active love towards the hate coming his way a "God-moment." Transformation came not by holding up a poster, shouting a slur, or making a speech that took a political position, but by loving someone who seemed, frankly, quite unlovable. It was a "living sermon." In the experience of that love, Furniss began to question his own motives.

The deep ache of the human heart is to be connected—connected to God and to one another. Bernard Levin, one of the greatest columnists of his generation, wrote an essay before his death in 2004 entitled "Life's Great Riddle and No Time to Find Its Meaning."

To put it bluntly, have I time to discover why I was born before I die? . . . I have not managed to answer that question yet, and however many years I have before me they are certainly not as many as there are behind. There is an obvious danger in leaving it too late . . . Why do I have to know why I was born? Because, of course, I am unable to believe that it was an accident, and if it wasn't one, it must have a meaning . . . Countries like ours are full of people who have all the material comforts they desire, together with such non-material blessings as a happy family, and yet lead lives of quiet, and at times noisy, desperation, understanding nothing but the fact that there is a hole inside them and that however much food and drink they pour into it, however many motor cars and television sets they stuff it with, however many well-balanced children and loyal friends they parade around the edges of it . . . it aches.

Ralph Barton, a successful cartoonist, left this note pinned to his pillow as he took his own life: "I have had few real difficulties. I have had an exceptionally glamorous life, as life goes; and I have had more than my fair share of affection and appreciation. [Yet,] I have run from wife to wife, from house to house and country to country in a ridiculous effort to escape from myself. . . . I am fed up with inventing devices for getting through twenty-four hours a day." Freddie Mercury, the lead singer of Queen, who died back in 1991, wrote in one of his last songs on *The Miracle* album, "Does anybody know what we are living for?" In spite of his success, fame, and wealth, he was desperately lonely. In an interview with the BBC not too long before his death, he shared, "You can have everything in the world and still be the loneliest man, and that is the most bitter type of loneliness. Success has brought me world idolization and millions of pounds, but it's prevented me from having the one thing we all need—a loving, ongoing relationship."

Augustine penned a line that would speak clearly to Levin, Barton, and Mercury—"My heart is restless until it rests in Thee."

The pulpit offers the pastor the unique ability to speak directly to the ache of the human heart. There are plenty of places where members of the human family can go to be prodded to think and act on their political persuasions, but the church can offer so much more. The pulpit, the sermon, and the preacher can speak to the deficiencies that cannot be satiated by the voting booth.

God Takes Center Stage

The reason humans find a spirituality or religion rooted in political structures lacking is that our core problems are not, in fact, political—they are spiritual. We are at odds with one another, because we are at odds with God. I once heard a phrase uttered by a poet at Christmastime that I will long remember, "There will be no peace on earth until each person, one by one, makes peace with God."

God is our only hope. The reconciliation provided us in Jesus Christ is the powerful medicine our divided culture, our divided churches, and our divided souls need. That is why the essential use of the pulpit must be to point to God's redemptive work in the life, death, and resurrection of Jesus. Fleming Rutledge, one of the best preachers of our time, argues in her masterful work *The Crucifixion* that if the Bible is to be understood in any way at all, it must be understood on its own terms: "From beginning to end, the principal acting subject is God."[4] Her claim is supported by the heart of Karl Barth's theological plumb line:

> The passion of Jesus Christ is the judgment of God in which the Judge Himself was the judged. And as such it is at its heart and center the victory which has been won for us, in our place, in the battle against sin. By this time it should be clear why it is so important to understand this passion as from the very first the divine action . . . the radical divine action which attacks and destroys at its very root the primary evil in the world; the activity of the second Adam who took the place of the first, who reversed and overthrew the activity of the first in this world, and in so doing brought in a new man, founded a new world and inaugurated a new aeon.[5]

If Rutledge and Barth are correct—and I believe they are—then the pressing need is for people to respond to God's action. As Rutledge

---

4. Fleming Rutledge, *The Crucifixion: Understanding the Death of Jesus Christ* (Grand Rapids: William B. Eerdmans, 2015), 523.

5. Karl Barth, *Church Dogmatics,* vol. IV (Edinburgh: T.&T. Clark, 1956–1975), 253–54.

notes, "We must not lose sight of the individual and the summons to the conversion and discipleship of individuals."[6]

Thus, the pulpit can be the primary launch pad from which people are called to reconciliation with God through conversion to Jesus Christ. Through that conversion, they can be transformed in a manner that ultimately bleeds out into the sick, sinful, and divided world in which we live, thereby accomplishing that which mere politics fails to do. Our preaching must be God-ward. This imperative was made clear by one of Anglicanism's great teachers and preachers, the late John Stott, in his book *The Cross of Christ.*

> God finished the work of reconciliation at the cross, yet it is still necessary for sinners to repent and believe and so "be reconciled to God." Again, sinners need to "be reconciled to God," yet we must not forget that on God's side the work of reconciliation has already been done. If these two things are to be kept distinct, they will also in all authentic gospel preaching be kept together. It is not enough to expound a thoroughly orthodox doctrine of reconciliation if we never beg people to come to Christ.[7]

Preaching must have the primary agenda of inviting others into a personal relationship with Jesus Christ as Lord and as Savior. This is the heart of the gospel. This and nothing more. Paul warned himself and all preachers: "Woe to me if I do not proclaim the gospel!" (1 Cor. 9:16) Perhaps this is an invitation for preachers to ask of themselves every time they preach, "Does this sermon call on my hearer to follow Jesus? Am I promoting love or inciting division? Am I preaching the gospel?" If not, then woe, indeed.

The Main Thing

It would be foolhardy to suggest that the gospel–the life, death, and resurrection of Jesus in the teachings of Scripture–is "simple" and easy to grasp. And yet, there are salient moments where it all seems to be clear, even simple. Think, for instance, of the thief on the cross next to

---

6. Rutledge, *Crucifixion*, 529.

7. John R. W. Stott, *The Cross of Christ*, 20th ed. (Downers Grove, IL: IVP, 2006), 198.

Jesus who utters, "Remember me when you come into your Kingdom," and Jesus's simple reply, "Truly I tell you, today you will be with me in paradise" (Luke 23:42–43). Jesus did not require a deep understanding of theology, subscription to a particular creed or code of conduct, denominational allegiance, or a liturgical act, only a heart desiring reconciliation to the One being crucified only steps away. Think also of Jesus's response when asked which were the greatest of all the laws. Jesus did not unpack a theory of ethics or deliver a complicated moral framework, nor did he suggest that a more hardy political structure or government overthrow was in order. Instead, he said, "Love God and love your neighbor."[8]

Another moment comes in Caesarea Philippi (Matthew 16:13–20). Jesus is about halfway through his earthly ministry. We know that by this point he is becoming increasingly frustrated with the religious hierarchy of his day. Despite his teaching and his miracles, so many still didn't get it. On this day, Jesus comes to the region of Caesarea Philippi, a city built by Herod's son Philip just north of the Sea of Galilee. Originally, it was called Panens, in honor of the Greek god Pan, whose shrine was located there. Jesus and his disciples had stepped into an especially pagan place. Perhaps it is for this reason that Jesus turned to his followers and asked the most important question of his ministry. The disciples were weary and, perhaps, like Jesus, frustrated. Jesus paused and they paused, too. Jesus looked them in the eye and asked, "Who do people say the Son of Man is?" Looking everywhere but at Jesus, they pondered, "John the Baptist, back from the dead. . . . Some say Elijah, . . . or one of the prophets." They reacted like school children scrambling to answer the teacher's question when none have studied the material.

Peter had not yet spoken and his eyes had not moved from the eyes of Christ. Jesus looked deeper, perhaps whispering, "What about you? Who do you say that I am?" Peter took a deep breath and responded, "You are the Christ, the Son of the living God." The speculation stopped, everyone looked from Peter to Jesus and waited for a response. Jesus answered, "Blessed are you Simon son of Jonah for this has been revealed to you by my Father in heaven!"

---

8. Luke 10:27 (paraphrased).

In one of the geographic hearts of paganism, and as the shadow of the Cross loomed ever closer, Jesus asked the question, "Who do you say that I am?"

By now, most of us have heard Stephen Covey's little phrase, "The main thing is to keep the main thing the main thing." I suppose in the corporate world, the "main thing" might be profit; in the entertainment world, it might be ratings; in the political world, it would likely be power. What about the Christian world? What is the main thing? That is precisely what Jesus was getting at in Caesarea Philippi. He was trying to tie up the loose ends and to bring clarity out of confusion. He was making sure that his disciples knew that, "the main thing was to keep the main thing the main thing." Nothing mattered more than the fact that the disciples knew their whole lives were to revolve around this person of Christ, the Son of the living God, Love incarnate, Jesus. That was "the main thing."

What does it say to twenty-first century preachers entrusted with the pulpit? Jesus's question is just as important now as it was then. We live in difficult, strange, perhaps even pagan, times. We have a culture that spends a lot of time talking about reconciliation. But, we cannot have reconciliation between polarized factions, be they races, political parties, or faith traditions, without God. That is what Jesus was getting at with his apostles in Caesarea Philippi. They wanted to be connected to God in a deeper way, but it was not going to happen without understanding that true reconciliation begins with the healing of the heart, and the healing of the heart begins with a commitment to Jesus Christ. To go back to that poetic phrase I referenced earlier, there will be no reconciliation on earth until each person—one by one—reconciles with God.

It is human to make of supreme importance a particular point of view. Are you liberal or conservative? Are you pro-choice or pro-life? Do you believe the Bible is literally true or not? Where do you stand on women's health issues? On same-sex marriage? On fracking? On what happened in the latest racial clash? These are important things, but these are not the main thing. Jesus stands steadfastly looking into our eyes and asking, "Who do you say that I am?" This, my friends, is the question for all humanity—not where you stand on this issue or that, but where you stand on Jesus.

The confession of Peter is the central faith of Christianity. In most churches, we say the ancient Nicene Creed in which are the words, "I believe in Jesus Christ, the Only Son of God." If we firmly believe that, we make not just an intellectual affirmation, but a "soul-trust," throwing ourselves into the hands of Christ for all eternity. Christ is the center: the funnel of the whirlpool, the eye of the storm, the foundation of our faith. Christ is Christianity.

Where is the hope for a world that seems almost daily to be spinning out of control? Where is the hope when our lives are in need of healing? Where did those early apostles turn for help with their messes and frustrations? The answer is in Peter's words: "Christ, the Son of the living God." This is the question that must be answered by the preacher, and this is the purpose of the pulpit today.

Remember Jesus

I titled my chapter, "Remember Jesus," because when those two words were spoken to me in the summer of 1990, they changed my outlook on ministry, teaching, and preaching. I had just finished up my first year of seminary at Virginia Theological Seminary in Alexandria, Virginia, when I was asked by a professor to drive to the local airport and pick up Krister Stendahl, the former bishop of Stockholm, a preeminent New Testament scholar, and, at the time, the chaplain at Harvard University.

I recall being anxious. I had one year of seminary under my belt. I was confident he might start quizzing me on the way back to the seminary campus. I actually arrived late and expected him to be a bit upset, but he did not even mention my tardiness. As we got in the car, he put me at ease. No questions on biblical languages, New Testament theory, or church history. In fact, it was a rather easy—simple is perhaps the better word—conversation. He wanted to get to know me. Once we got to campus, I realized I might not have a chance to ask this biblical scholar anything else one-on-one, so I asked him a single question.

"Dr. Stendahl, I've just finished up my first year of seminary and wonder if you have any advice for me." He thought for a minute and then in his thick Swedish accent said, "Yes. Remember Jesus. Remember Jesus and his cross. Today, all of our stories, all of our jokes, and all of our conversations are about the church, not Jesus. Remember Jesus."

From that day, every time I took notes I wrote the date and those two words, "Remember Jesus." Every time I wrote a letter to a friend, a fellow minister, a family member, a member of a church where I was serving, I would write the date and then the two words, "Remember Jesus."

A Closing Thought

I suppose something similar compelled Paul to write to the church in Corinth, so deeply divided in so many ways, such a simple reminder, "For I decided to know nothing among you except Jesus Christ, and him crucified" (1 Cor. 2:2). I am in my third, and I suspect my last, rectorship. In each place, I have had a small brass plaque with that scripture citation crafted and then placed on the pulpit. My hope is that every time someone climbs into one of those pulpits they are reminded of the power of those words. Even more, I hope they are reminded of the obligation to speak to the ache of the human heart by preaching Jesus Christ and him crucified. This is knowledge with the power to transform lives and reconcile people to God and to one another. This is the purpose of the pulpit, to preach so that the whole world might know that Jesus is God's son and that each and every one of us is loved by God, so that in God's time and in God's way, Jesus's prayer in Gethsemane might be answered.

The purpose of the pulpit? Remember Jesus. Lift up Jesus. Proclaim Jesus. He is the Good News. Sharing him should be the primary purpose of every preacher.

BIBLIOGRAPHY

Alcott, Louisa May. *An Old Fashioned Girl.* Boston: Little Brown, 1911.
Barth, Karl. *Church Dogmatics.* Vol. IV. Edinburgh: T.&T. Clark, 1956–1975.
Chia, Jessica. "Protester hugs Nazi outside Richard Spencer talk, asks 'Why do you hate me?'" *New York Daily News.* October 20, 2017. https://www.nydailynews.com/news/national/protester-hugged-nazi-pleads-hate-article-1.3575977.

Rutledge, Fleming. *The Crucifixion: Understanding the Death of Jesus Christ.* Grand Rapids: William B. Eerdmans, 2015.

Stott, John R.W. *The Cross of Christ.* 20th ed. Downers Grove, IL: IVP, 2006.

The Works of the Rev. John Wesley, A.M. Vol. 3. Entries for 24th and 29th of January, 1738. New York: Carlton & Porter, 1856.

Chapter 5

Reclaiming the Prophetic Pulpit

Alex Dyer

It is often suggested that progressive preaching is simply reflecting the trendy prejudices of liberal clergy ranting about the latest social justice issues. Sometimes, it feels like that; too often, progressive preachers fall woefully short of illustrating how their convictions are rooted in theology and scripture. How preachers view scripture may differ; nevertheless, preaching must be centered on the Good News of Christ.

The majority of people in the congregations I have served would likely categorize themselves as liberal or progressive. In some ways, I was more conservative than many members of my congregation. Nonetheless, the congregations who have called me have been more progressive parishes, partly because I am a married gay man with two kids. I know how to speak to progressive Christians, knowing what will make them comfortable and affirm their beliefs. Having spent many years in progressive parishes, I am also aware of some of the areas of growth.

No matter where our congregations fall on the political spectrum, we reflect our larger society. People are firmly entrenched in their views. Individuals rarely want to hear anything that contradicts what they believe to be the truth. In our lives outside of church, we cannot escape the constant assault of headlines. News networks are becoming increasingly partisan, and most of us choose a network that affirms our own preexisting beliefs. Pundits continuously vilify views that differ from their own as they shout at each other. Our conversations about important issues have been relegated to the online comment section of websites and social media, where we fall into familiar toxic patterns.

We are losing the ability to hold differing points of view and, therefore, many of us would rather just not have the conversation at all. At the risk of avoiding this uncomfortable pattern of behavior, many preachers choose not to address controversial issues. The question then is: can churches offer something different?

The Privilege of Determining the Prophetic, Political, or Pastoral

At the first parish where I was the priest-in-charge, I had lunch with one of my parishioners who occasionally attended on Sunday mornings. I questioned why he did not attend more regularly. He said that in large part it was due to my sermons. He thought that I challenged people too much. He said, "I come to church to feel good about myself. I don't come to be challenged." I know he is not alone. Many people in the pews (and even some in the pulpit) come to the church seeking refuge from the world. Many people crave the healing and wholeness that church offers in order to make it through the week.

In the 1960 film *Inherit the Wind*, Gene Kelly says, "Mr. Brady, it is the duty of a newspaper to comfort the afflicted and afflict the comfortable." Strangely enough, I was told this was the church's role. If it is the job of the media to comfort and to afflict, then what is the role of the church? Perhaps it is both the job of the media and the church to encourage discomfort with the status quo, but with each institution going about it in a different way. Both the media and the church claim to search out a deeper truth and to expose corruption; however, the church must do this through the lens of scripture and theology. The problem is that in some progressive congregations you cannot tell the difference between the headlines of the day and the sermon preached last Sunday.

If the church's sole reason for existence is not to comfort the afflicted and afflict the comfortable, then perhaps I am in the wrong profession. I cannot reconcile the alternative line of thinking with the Jesus I try to follow on a daily basis. If churches are simply to make people feel comfortable and not challenge the status quo, what is the point? If we define politics using Aristotle's definition—the "affairs of state"—the question is: should churches not have a voice in the public square? The church has an obligation and a calling to enter into people's lives as individuals and communally, as they strive for justice.

Dennis A. Jacobsen, in his book *Doing Justice: Congregations and Community Organizing,* argues that the church belongs in the public space because that is where Jesus did his ministry.

> The church enters the "this-worldliness" of the public arena because God is encountered in the encounter with those who suffer in the world. Jesus was born not in a church but in a stable. Jesus died, not of a heart attack from too many high cholesterol church dinners, but of crucifixion as an enemy of the Roman empire. The public arena is God's arena.[1]

Yet many church leaders across the Episcopal Church have argued that churches should stay out of politics, which generally means that we should shy away from controversial topics that could cause division in a congregation. To ignore politics is not to follow the way of Jesus found in scripture. As followers of Jesus, how can we remain silent as immigrant children are put in cages, high school children are being murdered in their schools, white nationalism is on the rise, and our current economy leads to an ever-widening gap between the ultra-wealthy and those who cannot make a living wage? Inherent in the choice of whether or not to engage these issues is privilege. Preachers have an incredible amount of privilege and power when crafting their sermons. Preachers have the luxury of addressing or ignoring a topic. Often the decision is based on how much conflict the preacher is willing to tolerate, or how passionate they feel about a particular issue.

We are called to be prophetic, but that does not make us all prophets. A gifted preacher knows their context. If a preacher has a good relationship with their congregation, the preacher will know when to challenge and when to comfort. Preachers cannot simply stand on a soap box and rant each Sunday, nor can they avoid the affairs of the state that weigh heavily on at least someone sitting in the pews. Preachers should also engage those times in history when God's Word needs to be preached. Every Sunday cannot be political or prophetic; however, there are some Sundays that must be prophetic. Fully engaging

---

1. D. A. Jacobsen, *Doing Justice: Congregations and Community Organizing* (Minneapolis: Fortress Press, 2017), 15.

the Good News of Jesus does not always make the preacher or the congregation feel comfortable.

Do Not Forget Where You Left Your Bible

The gospel is relevant to our current life issues and challenges as a society. Scripture is not a collection of metaphors or nice stories that have some kernel of wisdom. Scripture tells us about the relationship between God and God's people. As preachers, we cannot ignore what scripture is teaching us today and we should avoid preaching the latest social cause making the news. Our genesis is the Good News found in scripture, which is timeless.

As a denomination, I am worried about us becoming more progressive without bringing Jesus along with us. The Episcopal Church can be progressive and it can also hold firm to scripture and Orthodox theology. To do both requires an intentional choice to play by a different set of rules than our world offers. The Episcopal Church is at a crossroads, and we are making choices that will affect what kind of denomination we will be for the next generation.

Every three years the Episcopal Church gathers each diocese from the United States and beyond for its General Convention. I have had the opportunity to attend almost every convention since 2003. Over this time, I have witnessed good and faithful people wrestle with tough issues, including sexuality. For a variety of reasons, many people who identified as more traditional or conservative felt that they could no longer remain in the Episcopal Church and formed other denominations. The 2012 General Convention was the first convention without many of these conservatives in the room. Only a few conservative dioceses remained; some left the convention in protest to our legislative actions.

One of the main topics of discussion was the inclusion of transgender people in the life of the Episcopal Church, which I fully support. I am delighted that we made great strides in 2012 towards the full inclusion of transgender people. While I support where we ended up, I am not pleased with how we got there. I would argue that we can do better.

Many of my fellow progressive colleagues had grown tired of fighting for the inclusion of gay and lesbian people in the church. After decades of discussions, committees, and reports, progressives were anxious for action. Many people I talked to were relieved to finally move forward on this important issue. I noticed myself becoming frustrated with the debate from the convention floor. Perhaps this is an oversimplification, but much of the debate to include transgender people went something like, "Transgender people are good people, and we should include them in the life of the church." Or, "I know transgender people, and I like them. So, you should like them too." These are not direct quotes, but they sum up much of what I heard.

The few people who opposed the inclusion of transgender people cited scripture and theology. This debate was not unique in that people who opposed the resolution to include transgender people generally used scriptural evidence to back up their claim, as well as years of church tradition. The frustrating part of this debate was that in the rush to address transgender inclusion supporters did not cite scripture nor tradition in their statements for inclusion and acceptance. In the end, the resolution passed, and the Episcopal Church continued to march forward, as are other denominatons, making strides towards inclusion and building God's kingdom.

Because scripture and tradition were not cited as evidence in support of inclusion, it appears they don't support this position, which is unfortunate because they hold strong support of such a position. The debate could have centered on the stories of Genesis found in creation. But, it didn't. It did not talk about the views of many scholars who have argued that the Hebrew word for Adam was actually genderless until Eve was created. The words "man" and "woman" are not used until Genesis 2:21–22. It did not debate how God views gender or the meaning of Galatians 3:28. While there are many other sound theological arguments found in scripture and theology, the debate did not even begin to address them.

As the progressive voice in the Episcopal Church becomes louder, we need to challenge ourselves on *why* we are doing the things we are doing. Our *why* cannot be rooted in our own desires or in a need to keep up with the changing times. Scripture and church tradition are vital tools in framing *why* we value what we do, and the ability to articulate these supports is vital. There is a sound theological and scriptural foundation for the work that we are doing and we ignore it at our own peril.

Partisan Pundits in the Pulpit

Since the election of Donald Trump, mainline progressive churches have become more politically active. There is a renewed energy for action. No matter what political camp we may inhabit, the church's boldness and enthusiasm cannot be dependent on who occupies the White House, what party holds the majority in Congress, or the policies of a particular political party. Preachers who wrestle with scripture will inevitably find a time when scripture challenges or contradicts the status quo. Prophetic preachers are almost always at odds with the political or religious leaders at some point. No political party will usher in the kingdom of God.

Many preachers and parishioners believe that we have a common enemy and that this enemy is the person who is in an opposing political party or who may think and process the world differently than we do. When we fall victim to constructing shallow and false narratives about our neighbors who hold different views, we fall short of our call as Christians. Even when we are right, we often drift into smug self-righteousness. Liberal and conservative clergy can run the risk of being the same as the pundit on cable news who is convinced that their viewpoint is correct and that the opposing person does not understand. This lacks humility and compassion. It is rooted in sin.

One of the few good things I can say about our political climate is that it has awakened complacent and overconfident progressive mainline denominations across our country. The election of Donald Trump as the forty-fifth president of the United States, the Brexit vote in the United Kingdom, and growing autocracy around the globe have caused churches to reexamine the content of their message and how they preach.

How do leaders stand up for what they believe and remain rooted in humility and compassion? How do we stay true to scripture and our tradition? A great example is the presiding bishop of the Episcopal Church, the Most Rev. Michael Curry, who, along with other progressive Christian leaders, is reclaiming the name of Jesus for the progressive voice. Presiding Bishop Curry and other prominent faith leaders came together in 2017 to write a letter expressing a desire for Christians to reclaim Jesus.

When politics undermine our theology, we must examine those politics. The church's role is to change the world through the life and love of Jesus Christ. The government's role is to serve the common good by protecting justice and peace, rewarding good behavior while restraining bad behavior (Romans 13). When that role is undermined by political leadership, faith leaders must stand up and speak out. Rev. Dr. Martin Luther King Jr. said, "The church must be reminded that it is not the master or the servant of the state, but rather the conscience of the state."

It is often the duty of Christian leaders, especially elders, to speak the truth in love to our churches and to name and warn against temptations, racial and cultural captivities, false doctrines, and political idolatries—and even our complicity in them. We do so here with humility, prayer, and a deep dependency on the grace and Holy Spirit of God.[2]

Progressive leaders are speaking the truth in love. Finding the balance of speaking truth to power and speaking the truth in love is a difficult road to navigate. Too often, we want to speak our truth and forget the love, or we are so worried about offending our siblings that we do not speak the truth. If we are to be the "conscience of the state," then followers of Jesus need to stand up for what is right and just and not get caught up in partisan politics. Sound theology and grounding in scripture help keep us from seeking our own desires instead of God's desire.

God can offer a different way. We have the unique call of not only speaking to current events, but also inviting people into a new future. Political pundits deal with the present; prophets call us to hope for what God has in store. Biblical texts speak to both truth and hope in a profound way and we cannot ignore either. This hope is defiant and available now for those who want to take a risk and follow God.

Jesus and the State Department

Every congregation I have served required me to speak and act differently. I was myself and there were commonalties in every place, but the different congregations needed to hear different things. With my most recent congregation in the heart of Washington, DC, I know how

---

2. "Reclaiming Jesus: a Confession of Faith in a Time of Crisis," Reclaiming Jesus, accessed April 11, 2019, http://www.reclaimingjesus.org.

seductive secular power can be to followers of Jesus, myself included. The Episcopal Church has also had an interesting relationship with institutions and our government even before the birth of our nation.

For centuries, the Episcopal Church has benefited from having a disproportionate representation in all branches of our government. There have been more Episcopal presidents than any other denomination despite the fact that, historically, we have had no more than a few million members, even at the height of the denomination's popularity. We have always had a large number of parishioners in Congress, and there have been numerous Supreme Court justices who were Episcopalians.

Many people in the Episcopal Church have viewed the denomination as the de facto national church. Dwight J. Zscheile, in *People of the Way: Renewing Episcopal Identity,* notes, "Perhaps the most visible expression of the 'national church' sense of Episcopal identity and mission is the construction of Washington National Cathedral (begun in 1907, completed in 1990), representing from its perch high above the capital the Christian values that were assumed to underpin the nation."[3] The Episcopal Church saw its role and purpose as sanctifying society from the center, with access to power and privilege like few other denominations. The price for this access has often meant rarely challenging our government. Instead, Episcopalians have viewed themselves as slowly guiding our country.

Congress passed the charter bill in December 1892; it was signed on January 6, 1893, by President Benjamin Harrison. The charter created and gave powers to the "Protestant Episcopal Cathedral Foundation" to "establish and maintain within the District of Columbia a cathedral and institutions of learning for the promotion of religion, education and charity."[4] The "National Cathedral" has become a source of pride for many Episcopalians during state funerals and times of national

---

3. Dwight J. Zscheile, *People of the Way: Renewing Episcopal Identity* (New York: Morehouse, 2012), 24.

4. "Key Dates and Events," About Us, Protestant Episcopal Cathedral Foundation, accessed April 11, 2019, https://pecf.org/about-us/18-about-us/38-board-of-trustees.

tragedy. The cathedral has served this nation in many ways, yet there have been times when it has also been a cause for division.

A recent example is the prayer service for then newly-elected President Donald Trump. While predecessors had similar services at the National Cathedral, many Episcopalians were outraged that our National Cathedral—an Episcopal church—would hold such a service. They felt that President Trump's policies were at odds with Christian values. Many struggled with what they believed was the National Cathedral explicitly condoning President Trump's rhetoric and actions during the 2016 campaign.

In response to these concerns, the Episcopal bishop of Washington, the Right Reverend Mariann Budde, called for the Diocese of Washington to form a task force to examine the role of the National Cathedral in our current society. Nearly a year after Donald Trump's inauguration, this task force held a listening session that I attended. I proposed that the cathedral drop the reference of National Cathedral and refer to itself by its other name: the Cathedral of St. Peter and St. Paul. The reaction to my proposed change was a bit surprising. One task force member wondered out loud what relationship the cathedral would then have with the State Department. Such a question is something that most churches do not have to worry about for obvious reasons. I asked a follow-up question in response: "I wonder what Jesus's relationship with the State Department would be?"

Imbedded in the conversation about our National Cathedral is a centuries-old argument about the relationship between the church and the state. Anglican theologian Richard Hooker represents one side. He argued that church and state are unified. He could not reconcile Puritans who claimed to be loyal to the queen while not supporting her church. In Hooker's mind, the people of England were all Anglican and pledged to serve the queen, who was the head of state and the supreme authority of the church. Christian socialist F.D Maurice promoted a church that could reform government using Christian principles. One side might represent the prophet Nathan, who rebuked King David as a member of his council, and the other side might be a prophet like John the Baptist, who rebuked Herod and ended up with his head on a plate. As Christianity once again debates the role of the church in our society, the National Cathedral is a lightning rod for those on either side of the debate.

Let us return to my question about Jesus and the State Department. I would argue that Jesus would not care too much about what the State Department thought of him. Christ knew his mission and was willing to live out that mission no matter what the cost. Christ was continuing in a long line of prophets who were centered in the narrative of God and prepared to sacrificially follow God wherever the path leads.

Preachers across this country still choose to play it safe and not challenge the status quo. This is in part because we value our robust pension plans and our desire for sufficient pledge income to pay our salaries. Or because we know we need support in an upcoming capital campaign. In other words, the desire to preach prophetically is thwarted because of our own corruption and complicity in an unjust system.

We must examine our own complicity in perpetuating a status quo that is all too often at odds with God's intention for God's creation. This makes most preachers uncomfortable (or should make them uncomfortable), and we are forced to realize that we are not immune from fear of engaging in these realities. It is much easier to choose to sanitize scripture to make it more palatable for our congregations. Disrupting our own status quo is often difficult and painful. It is hard to be a prophet when you are on the payroll.

Many preachers are not as concerned about the status quo because they serve congregations who share their political views. These preachers are encouraged by their people and even pressed onward at times. It is tempting to rail against what is in the latest headline. However, no matter what the context, sermons are not about the preacher and their opinions or political biases.

Prophet or Prophetic?

If prophetic preaching is rooted in the prophets found in scripture, then the messages are not about personal agendas but God's agenda. They are sermons in which the preacher is the least significant player. They allow the message to come across with minimal contamination by their opinions and biases. I talked once with a former parishioner about a colleague who was one of the best preachers I had heard.

We were trying to put our finger on what made his sermons so great. His delivery was above average, but nothing spectacular. Then the parishioner said something that I have tried to incorporate into my own preaching. She said, "In his sermons, he was never the hero of his stories. You always felt you were right there with him trying to figure it all out and not necessarily getting it right." Preachers are at their best when they are not simply articulate and authoritative pontificators, but are companions who struggle to understand who God is in their life and help others do the same.

The challenge with prophetic preaching is to avoid the appearance of an overly-righteous individual trying to transform a corrupt and primitive system. Whether preacher, prophet, or both, we all need to be grounded in our communities, both inside and outside the walls of the church. A preacher cannot simply read the headlines or listen to their favorite political pundit and then connect that with scripture.

If we trace the role of prophets throughout scripture then we see a movement towards a more communal model. As Episcopalians, we often emphasize the Incarnation of Jesus. When we hear of grand speeches by biblical heroes, we forget that these people lived among the people to whom they preached. We read their words handed down to us, but we must pay attention to the context–the relationships that were established over time. Prophets and preachers are at their best when the community is engaged both prophetically and pastorally. Prophets were not sent to simply rail against an outside community. They were called to resist from within their own communities and their own people.

Challenging another community is easier than challenging your own people, but sometimes it is necessary to be a prophet in one's hometown. Challenging your own community is the difficult call that preachers can choose to embrace. Confrontational preaching rarely wins a popularity contest. If a preacher is not seen as preaching with people, then they may be seen as preaching at people. In order for the prophetic word to be heard and integrated into the lives of their congregation, a preacher must know their community and be willing to continue the conversation beyond the sermon.

Perhaps prophetic preaching looks, or could look, different in a progressive or liberal church. A more communal model could be the voice of the progressive churches, if we are willing to claim it. We cannot simply be churches that react to the injustices of the world as if we were somehow more righteous and not a part of the injustice. We are called to be companions along the way with those who question and challenge us all to be more faithful followers of Christ. For far too long, conservative and evangelical Christians have chosen to claim the mantle of being the prophetic voice of Christianity. Evangelical and conservative preachers have never shied away from social issues and have spoken with a moral authority that has been absent in more progressive churches.

Many charismatic figures have taken the stance of the morally righteous individual who has come to redeem a corrupt society. These mostly conservative-leaning preachers have seen themselves as against the community and larger society, and morally superior to the established norms. Many see this individualistic model as the only model for prophetic preaching. Some progressive congregations even crave this model, desiring ammunition to use against those who disagree with them. Liberal churches are called to confront their own demons and biases in order to have a fruitful and productive conversation about differing opinions and the complexities of society.

The truth is that people who choose to follow Jesus and to be transformed by Jesus know the richness of Christianity. Even today, people think that Christianity is individualistic, narrow minded, homophobic, and maybe even racist. Each time we choose to remain silent about these and other issues we are complicit in allowing these perceptions to persist and even to thrive.

Measure the Cost

I still remember the Sunday when Matthew 5:31–32 was a part of the gospel reading in one congregation where I served. That is the passage about divorce, which appears harsh and cruel to the modern ear. One of my colleagues chose not to engage the text and to play it safe. At the conclusion of the service, I saw a long-time parish leader in tears, and, knowing her history, I knew why. She had recently gone through a difficult divorce and her ex-husband continued to worship in the same parish. Divorce is complicated and messy for sure and an unfortunate part of life at times. I am not saying the preacher should have talked about their particular situation, but neglecting the subject, in this instance, did not help that woman. Preachers who choose to ignore a difficult passage of scripture rather than acknowledging its complexity and framing it within a scriptural and theological context often do more harm than good. The intent was to gloss over a difficult subject, but the impact was painful for those who had experienced the situation.

To believe that people are not wrestling with political and social issues is naive. People bring all the challenges of the world into churches across America each day. By staying silent on these complex issues, preachers are implicitly saying that God does not care about them. Like my former parishioner, we create our own narratives. This can be especially true in progressive parishes where the voice of progressive Christianity is not as loud as more conservative Christian narratives.

I think about the gay, lesbian, queer, bisexual, or transgender person who has been told their whole life that God hates them or that God made a mistake. At my first church, I coordinated the outreach ministries, which included a Saturday program for LGBTQ youth, most of whom were living on the streets. One Saturday, a group of teens entered the back entrance of the school that was attached to the church building. When one of the young people saw me in my clerical collar, he exclaimed, "Hold up! Is this a church? I thought the church hated us." No, I thought. The church does not hate you. Luckily, I was able to show him something different that day.

I remember talking with youth most Saturdays who were convinced that God hated them and quoted scripture that had been used against them their whole lives. I tried to show them another God in scripture—a God who loved them more than they could imagine. Even after all of these years, I still encounter people who have been beaten up by other churches because of their gender, gender identity, sexual orientation, or whatever stereotype you want to place on a person. There are plenty of people willing to speak for Jesus, and all too often the words they use push people away from God.

To preach in this moment, or any moment in history, and not identify with intentional clarity and boldness the kinds of political, social, and economic realities that contradict Jesus and his teachings is no longer an option. As preachers, we must willingly and wholeheartedly engage any perceived contradiction to the purposes of God and declare that these practices will come to no good. We do not have to have all the answers, but we are called to ask the challenging questions, to listen, and to act. Inevitably, there will be times where the scripture speaks to our present reality in a way we cannot ignore.

The world needs to hear from well-grounded and scripture-centered progressive Christian leaders. Conservative Christians cannot be the only voice in the public square. Who knows what the future holds for churches, wherever they fall on the political spectrum? It is my prayer that every church, and preacher, will continue to wrestle with scripture and with the concerns that are going on in people's lives today. It is my hope that more liberal churches will continue to find their voice in the public square.

I cannot think of a prophet who did not struggle with the call to speak for God to a broken world. The task of any preacher is to pick up this mantle and to build upon those who have gone before to declare hope and salvation to this generation. Liberal churches cannot be silent anymore. As Jesus entered Jerusalem, it says that "some of the Pharisees in the crowd said to him, 'Teacher, order your disciples to stop.' Jesus answered, 'I tell you, if these were silent, the stones would shout out'" (Luke 19:39–40). My prayer is that preachers will not listen to the modern Pharisees and will instead shout out the Good News of God working in our world today.

BIBLIOGRAPHY

Jacobsen, D. A. *Doing Justice: Congregations and Community Organizing*. Minneapolis: Fortress Press, 2017.

Protestant Episcopal Cathedral Foundation, "Key Dates and Events." About Us. Accessed April 11, 2019. https://pecf.org/about-us/18-about-us/38-board-of-trustees.

"Reclaiming Jesus: A Confession of Faith in a Time of Crisis." Reclaiming Jesus. Accessed April 11, 2019. http://www.reclaimingjesus.org.

Zscheile, Dwight J. *People of the Way: Renewing Episcopal Identity*. New York: Morehouse, 2012.

Chapter 6

Preaching the Jesus Movement

Stephanie Spellers

If you are concerned about preaching a potentially politically charged message in our current divided age, then preaching the Jesus Movement[1] would seem to present a particular challenge. The very word—"movement"—insinuates that trouble is brewing. Add Jesus to the mix and you are almost guaranteed to upset someone. Yet, I would suggest here that both prophetic preaching and the Jesus Movement are among the basics of Christian life. The question is not whether to preach prophetically, or whether to proclaim the Jesus Movement, it is only how.

We Are Movement People

Even before he was elected as our twenty-seventh presiding bishop, Michael B. Curry was challenging Episcopalians to understand ourselves—not just as the Episcopal Church, but as the Episcopal branch of the Jesus Movement. Along the way, many have been energized and intrigued by the idea, while some have bristled. Movement language, even with Jesus at the front, can sound distinctly partisan. After all, isn't a movement an action against or away from another group? It does not need to be that way.

As Bishop Curry explains in the opening chapters of *Following the Way of Jesus*, the Jesus Movement is not some marginal or contemporary expression of church life. It establishes the essence of Christian identity.

This Jesus Movement isn't a twenty-first-century invention or a throwback to 1960s "Jesus Freaks" or a rhetorical concoction of my making. We're talking about going forward as a church by going

---

1. https://www.episcopalchurch.org/jesus-movement.

back to our deepest roots as disciples of Jesus Christ. New Testament scholars and others who look at early Christian origins often refer to the Christian movement in its beginnings as the "Jesus Movement." . . . When we use the phrase the "Jesus Movement," we're actually pointing back to the earliest days of Jesus's teaching and his followers moving in his revolutionary footsteps in the power of the Spirit. Together with them, we're following Jesus and growing a loving, liberating, life-giving relationship with God, with each other, and with the earth.[2]

Later in the book, Curry describes the Jesus Movement in clear terms. It is, he says, the "community of people whose lives are constantly being reoriented around Jesus, bearing witness to his way, not the world's way. We are living his way of love, not our own."[3]

The idea of Christianity as the movement initiated by Jesus is familiar to biblical scholars like Elisabeth Schüssler Fiorenza and Rodney Stark. Even before these scholars offered their take, Clarence Jordan, a well-trained student of the Bible and a passionate early advocate for civil rights in the American South, claimed Jesus was inaugurating a movement.

I am increasingly convinced that Jesus thought of his messages as not dead-ending in a static institution but as a mighty flow of spirit which would penetrate every nook and cranny of man's personal and social life. . . . I really don't think we can ever renew the church until we stop thinking of it as an institution and start thinking of it as a movement.[4]

Jordan helps us to fundamentally recast the relationship of movement to Christianity. He knows how churches have emphasized stasis over change, the old over the new, firm grounding over shifting realities. It took guts for him to suggest that movement is more true to the heart of

---

2. Michael B. Curry, *Following the Way of Jesus* (New York: Church Publishing, 2017), 1–2.

3. Ibid., 11–12.

4. Charles Marsh, *The Beloved Community: How Faith Shapes Social Justice, from the Civil Rights Movement to Today* (New York: Basic Books, 2005), 81.

Christianity than institution, and that the institution exists to serve the movement, and not the other way around.

This is still dangerous ground for congregational leaders, especially for those who preach in Episcopal congregations where we pride ourselves on the *via media*–a middle way that does not lean heavily into one extreme or the other. How can we welcome people to the Jesus Movement without seeming to dismiss centuries of tradition and faith? How can a church that prefers conservation over movement begin to shift without alienating half the people in the pews?

Here is the biblical truth: Jesus never founded an institution, and, even if he had, it would not be an institution that stood still. Nothing about the path of Jesus or those who follow him is static. In John 1:39, Jesus calls disciples with the words, "Come and see." In the other three Gospels, he says, "Follow me." In Matthew 4:17, he calls people to "repent, for the kingdom is at hand." That word "repent"–*metanoia*–means to turn. In other words, Jesus went about the highways and byways announcing, "Whatever you've been doing, whatever direction you've been walking, whatever love you've been pursuing, I'm asking you to do something else, go somewhere else, love something bigger. It's time to turn."

Those who followed Jesus never stopped moving. At the end of the Gospels, Jesus sent his first disciples out with the word, "Go." He tells them to "Go therefore and make disciples of all nations" (Matt. 28:19). He urges them to "Go into all the world and proclaim the good news to the whole creation" (Mark 16:15). After his crucifixion and resurrection, Jesus is still on the move and sending others out. He tells the gathered disciples, "[Y]ou will receive power when the Holy Spirit has come upon you; and you will be my witnesses in Jerusalem, in all Judea and Samaria, and to the ends of the earth" (Acts 1:8).

It may feel uncomfortable. It may not be our wish. But if we are Christian, we follow a God who is on the move. More than that, we are made in the image of this moving God. We are called to be movement people.

Church leaders are sure to experience pushback, resentment, and even punishment from people who want to stay exactly where they are. So much of church culture is about reassuring people that the world may change but the church will always be the same. Leaders may be pulling a resistant people to heed God's call to *move*. Somewhat unfortunately, we think being pastoral is being kind and keeping things on an even keel.

It would be far wiser to turn our collective eye to John 15, where Jesus gives his disciples a prescription for navigating rocky, changing times with their faith intact:

> *Abide in me as I abide in you. Just as the branch cannot bear fruit by itself unless it abides in the vine, neither can you unless you abide in me. I am the vine, you are the branches. Those who abide in me and I in them bear much fruit, because apart from me you can do nothing.*
>
> *John 15:4–5*

The Jesus Movement is rooted *in Jesus*. We abide in him, taking up the practices and commitments he promised would keep us connected to him, like branches to the vine. As part of the Jesus Movement, we turn from our own selfish ways and toward Jesus. We learn his story and his ways in scripture. We pray to the God with whom he ushers us into intimate relationship. We worship and place God at the center of our lives. We bless the world with our resources, time, and love. We go across boundaries to form beloved community. We rest and continue to abide in the grace and power of God. This Way of Love[5] is our rock, our stronghold. Being the Episcopal branch of the Jesus Movement is simply living as the extension—the branch—off the one true vine who is God revealed among us. That One is Jesus.

Some of the commitments and practices along the Way of Love may look political or partisan, but that is only because some groups have leaned into certain of those commitments and practices while eschewing the rest. Growing a life of prayer may seem irrelevant to some people who are oriented to public action and social transformation. Blessing and healing the least of these may place us at odds with the powers of this world (some of whom sit in the pews). Crossing boundaries of gender, race, culture, and class may make us look radical to our neighbors. That does not mean our actions are political. If they are political, if we are taking sides, it is only because we have first taken the side of the gospel—the side our Lord Jesus Christ has already staked out.

---

5. Learn more about the seven practices that comprise the Way of Love at www. episcopalchurch.org/wayoflove.

Presiding Bishop Michael Curry so often reminds us that Jesus did not come to found a church; he came to start a movement. Being movement people—and preaching so that people find their place in the movement—is the natural, inevitable outcome of following Jesus. Our Lord was on the move. We cannot be his people unless we are moving too.

We Are Prophetic People

My partner Albert is a school teacher in Harlem. In preparing for a recent unit covering Martin Luther King Jr.'s "Letter from a Birmingham Jail," he sat at the dining table and asked me, "So, what do I need to know about prophets?" It gave us both a chance to look at the popular understanding of prophets, along with the biblical and social reality.

Technically, a prophet is "a person regarded as an inspired teacher or proclaimer of the will of God."[6] A prophet also "predicts, or claims to be able to predict, what will happen in the future."[7] As we kept hunting, we saw that "prophet" usually traces to the Hebrew word אִיבָנ (navi), or "spokesperson." This is most clear in Deuteronomy 18:18, where God says, "I will put my words in his mouth, and he shall speak unto them all that I shall command him." Basically, the navi was the "mouth" of God, someone who opened to become a vessel pouring forth whatever message God wanted the people to receive.

So, prophets are first and foremost people who speak a word from God. They may call out the things that run afoul of the will of God. They will often warn about what's on the horizon—usually something the audience isn't keen to hear. More often than not, they are only following the current trajectory to its logical conclusion or reminding people of consequences God has already made plain. They will speak truth to power, not to be a gadfly, but because the powerful hold control over the systems that must be redeemed, transformed, or even overthrown in order for God's dream to become reality.

A priest friend directed me to another helpful text: 1 Corinthians 14. Paul offers a popular teaching about speaking in tongues here, so most

---

6. Judy Pearsall, ed., *The New Oxford Dictionary of English* (New York: Oxford, 1998), 1487.

7. Ibid., 1487.

readers have missed the rest of the story. Read more closely, and you will notice that he has equal zeal for cultivating the spiritual gift of prophecy:

> *Pursue love and strive for the spiritual gifts, and especially that*
> *you may prophesy. For those who speak in a tongue do not speak*
> *to other people but to God; for nobody understands them, since*
> *they are speaking mysteries in the Spirit. On the other hand, those*
> *who prophesy speak to other people for their upbuilding and*
> *encouragement and consolation. Those who speak in a tongue build*
> *up themselves, but those who prophesy build up the church.*
>
> 1 Cor. 14:1–4

The prophet's chief role is not just to speak a difficult word. Prophets have to speak in a way that edifies the church and the community within which God has called them to prophesy. A hard word that willfully angers or alienates people without a measure of hope and encouragement is no better than speaking in tongues without inter-pretation—a clanging cymbal, a ringing gong, signifying nothing and serving no one.

The more Albert and I learned about prophets and the prophetic mes-sage, the more I began to think both have been woefully (and perhaps willfully) misunderstood. The prophet is no shady figure on the edge of the church's life; it would seem that we are all meant to be prophets.

Walter Brueggemann is known for presenting the prophetic in main-stream Christian spaces that would like nothing more than to shove it to the margins. In a recent *Sojourners* interview with Kenyatta Gilbert, Brueggemann revisited his definition of a prophet:

> A prophet is someone that tries to articulate the world as though God were really active in the world. And that means, on the one hand, to identify those parts of our world order that are contradic-tory to God, but on the other hand, it means to talk about the will and purpose that God has for the world that will indeed come to fruition even in circumstances that we can't imagine.[8]

8. Walter Brueggemann, interview by Kenyatta Gilbert, "What Does It Mean to Be Prophetic Today?," *Sojourners,* accessed on April 9, 2019, https://sojo.net/media/what-does-it-mean-be-prophetic-today.

Brueggemann helps us to imagine the two sides of the prophetic: lament and hope, critique and embrace. Kenyatta Gilbert, an African American scholar who wrote *Exodus Preaching,* responds to Brueggemann with his own take: "A prophet is someone who sees that this is not all there is, but is willing to face the fact that we are in a predicament and it's only as we co-participate with God, can we find ourselves moving in the direction of a beloved community."[9]

The prophet sees things as they are and as they could be. More specifically, prophets see things as they are and as *God* would have them be. They have cultivated the space within to truly hear and receive God's word, and they help others to imagine and step into a more God-centered way of being. If this sounds like the yin-yang of Brueggemann's lament and hope, that is fitting. Both elements—the painful reality of the current day, the shimmering hope of God's dream—should be fully embodied in any instance of true preaching.

In light of the wisdom of scripture, tradition, and current experience, I have come to three conclusions about prophecy in general and prophetic preaching in particular.

1. The prophetic has gotten a bad rap. Most mainline church folk think of the prophetic as liberal, harsh, contrarian, or unreasonable. Is it? Or, is that just what the powerful and comfortable say about the prophetic? It makes perfect sense that, if you have benefitted from the skewed system, you will grumble about the corrective prophecy and the prophet who delivers it. Unfortunately, privileged people get to write the history and skew everyone else's conception of what is prophetic. In reality, the prophet is speaking a word from God, a word that is meant to re-order life for a community that has drifted from the will of God. That word may rankle the feathers of those of us for whom the system works. That doesn't make the prophecy any less true or godly.

2. All authentic preaching is prophetic. If I've simply made up the word I'm speaking, if I have not abided deeply in Christ and sought to be grafted to his one true vine, I may be a crafty speaker, but I am not a Christian prophet. If the word is God-inspired

---

9. Ibid.

and God-saturated, then it is prophetic. It will, as some might say, smell like God. If it does not—if it smells like Stephanie but cannot be traced to the Spirit of God and the gospel of Jesus Christ—then the congregation has every reason to tune it out.

3. Prophets do more than speak truth to power, drop the mic, and walk away. Prophets seek to edify, form, and transform. "Otherwise," the apostle Paul points out, "if you say a blessing with the spirit, how can anyone in the position of an outsider say the 'Amen' to your thanksgiving, since the outsider does not know what you are saying? For you may give thanks well enough, but the other person is not built up" (1 Cor. 14:15–17). Moral superiority, righteous indignation, and bitterness cannot drive us, however powerful and seductive they may be. While the prophet does not seek the affirmation of the crowds, she does not read their disaffection or anger as a good sign. She prays and discerns the *via media,* that middle path where people can hear at least some of the message, even if they disagree or disavow its implications for their comfortable lives.

These insights point me toward a conclusion: neither the Jesus Movement nor prophetic preaching is optional for those who would serve Jesus and call others to follow him. The question is not whether prophetic preaching and the Jesus Movement matter. The question is how to effectively and faithfully embrace both.

BIBLIOGRAPHY

Brueggemann, Walter. Interview by Kenyatta Gilbert, "What Does It Mean to Be Prophetic Today?" *Sojourners.* Accessed on April 9, 2019. https://sojo.net/media/ what-does-it-mean-be-prophetic-today.

Curry, Michael B. *Following the Way of Jesus.* New York: Church Publishing, 2017.

Marsh, Charles. *The Beloved Community: How Faith Shapes Social Justice, from the Civil Rights Movement to Today.* New York: Basic Books, 2005.

Pearsall, Judy, ed. *The New Oxford Dictionary of English.* New York: Oxford, 1998.

Chapter 7

The Political Work of the Church
Go for the Underlying Issues

Ian S. Markham

It is all so tempting. A news story provokes outrage. The rector is looking at the Old Testament lesson from Micah: "He has told you, O mortal, what is good; and what does the Lord require of you but to do justice, and to love kindness, and to walk humbly with your God?" (6:8). The next Sunday, the rector moves from this text to a denunciation of the injustice.

What is the result? The liberals love the sermon; the conservatives feel alienated. Some of the conservatives decide to leave. Pledges fall. They do not want the pulpit to be turned into a platform for the *New York Times*. No one's mind is changed. The net result is a damaged community.

Yet many clergy in the mainline are taking the risk. We are haunted by our inadequate response to the civil rights campaign of the 1960s. The churches were not at the vanguard of this crucial moment for justice. Too many feared disruptions in their congregations, so they tolerated implicit racism (sometimes, even, explicit racism) and did not stand with the civil rights movement. Some congregations were even part of the opposition to civil rights. Charles Marsh, in his powerful study *God's Long Summer*, documents the opposition of the church to the civil rights movement. He writes of Douglas Hudgins, the theologian of the closed society, that he "preached a gospel of individual salvation and personal orderliness, construing civil rights activism as not only a defilement of social purity but even more as simply irrelevant to the proclamation of Jesus Christ as God."[1] As a Baptist minister, Hudgins saw faith as all about individual salvation and pleasant civic participation. Marsh asserts, "It is no exaggeration to say that one can simply not understand white indifference to black suffering and liberation during the civil rights movement without understanding the religion of William Douglas Hudgins."[2] Although rectors of Episcopal congregations were more nuanced, many were complicit. Such congregations have been judged harshly by history. The inability to see the moral imperative of the moment was a grave deficiency.

Despite the danger of congregational division, some are arguing that prophetic preaching is an obligation. Perhaps the best illustration is O. Wesley Allen Jr. In *Preaching in the Era of Trump*, he advocates for sermons that confront explicitly the issues of race, gender, LGBT issues, and Islam. While he concedes that there were reluctant Trump voters (those who feared a President Hillary Clinton or wanted conservative jurists on the Supreme Court), he takes the view that any enthusiastic supporter of President Trump needs to be challenged; no faithful Christian with integrity could have voted for Donald Trump. He concludes:

> The church must heed God's call and not let Trump's bigotry and hatred be the loudest voice of the day. This is an opportunity for preachers to claim the mantle that Trump has unintentionally laid on our shoulders and reclaim the pulpit as a place where prophecy is heard.[3]

In my judgment, this is too simplistic. It does not work hard enough to read the moment; it does not assess the complexities of the moment; and it does not seek to confront the underlying factors behind a populist movement.

So how do we get this right? In this chapter, I will argue that preaching must always be set in the eternal context and that sometimes this

---

1. Charles Marsh, *God's Long Summer* (Princeton, NJ: Princeton University Press, 1997), 89.

2. Ibid., 114.

3. O. Wesley Allen Jr., *Preaching in the Era of Trump* (St. Louis: Chalice Press, 2017), 110.

does require a prophetic dimension. The steps in the argument are as follows. First, we should start with the appropriate capacity to "read the signs of the time." We need to distinguish between a policy disagreement and an eternal moral imperative. In this section, I argue that we are seeing a reaction to the adverse impact of globalization on certain communities. Second, linked to the issue of globalization, we should allow for the deep emotional ties that some people feel as they fear the mobility of labor. Third, we should preach to address underlying anxieties and dispositions that often create inappropriate political instincts. And, finally, from time to time one should address a political moment but do so sure of its eternal significance. I will now address each element in turn.

Reading the Signs of the Times

You know how to interpret the appearance of the sky, but you cannot interpret the signs of the times.

                                                            Matthew 16:3

Making sense of our political moment is always a difficult task. There is nothing easy about interpreting the complexity of this or that movement, but a preacher must do this hard work. The work of connecting the written word and the Eternal Word with the proclaimed word is a work of attending to the needs of a congregation and the signs of the times. This means that a preacher needs to read widely and think deeply.

The recent rise of populist movements around the globe (the election of President Trump, Brexit, the rise of Alternative for Germany, for example) illustrates that there are concerns about globalization, which run counter to the key messages of the last twenty years, where defenders of globalization celebrated the following:

1. In 1964, 64 percent of the world's population lived in extreme poverty, in 2015, it is less than 10 percent;

2. In 1960, 58 percent of the world's population were illiterate, in 2014, the number is 15 percent;

3. And developing companies have seen positive change—in India in 1990, 338 million people were living on less than a dollar a

day, by 2013 it was 218 million; in Brazil, the numbers moved from 31 million to 10 million; in Indonesia, the numbers moved from 104 million to 25 million; and in China, the numbers shifted from 756 million to 25 million.[4]

The problem is that much of this achievement has been fueled by an unprecedented credit boom. Therefore, Ian Bremmer has argued that 2008 was the pivotal year when the weak foundations of this achievement were exposed. The debt crisis of 2008 was the end of a debt-fueled global expansion. Although globalization had reduced poverty, there was growing inequality of rewards. Therefore, "incomes for the bottom half of earners in the United States remained flat between 1980 and 2014, while income for the top 0.001 percent of the richest Americans surged a jaw dropping 636 percent."[5] This, coupled with technology, meant that there was a significant erosion of lower-paid positions. No longer was there any confidence that one's children would be better off than their parents. This global backdrop needs to be taken seriously.

Bremmer is right to assert, "No one voted for Donald Trump because he believed the United States was growing more secure and more prosperous. In a country where working-age men without jobs outnumber those with jobs by three to one and half of the unemployed men take daily pain medication, a lot of people want 'change.'"[6] We need to see the complexity here. Bremmer continues:

Many Trump voters, including those who once supported Barack Obama, backed him because they wanted change. Actual change, not the kind of change promised on campaign posters. There's a working class in the United States that really has seen more losses than gains from free trade. U.S. infrastructure is crumbling, the country's education system is underperforming, its health care system is in real trouble, and the U.S. penal system doesn't work. American soldiers have fought and died in wars that seemed to accomplish nothing and that were never adequately explained to

4. These statistics are taken from Ian Bremmer, *Us Vs. Them: The Failure of Globalism* (London: Portfolio Penguin, 2018), 37.

5. Bremmer, *Us Vs. Them: The Failure of Globalism,* 27.

6. Ibid., 161.

the American people. These failures belong to the entire U.S. political establishment. Citizens feel lied to or ignored—by politicians, the mainstream media, the business elite, bankers, and public intellectuals. They believe the game is rigged in someone else's favor, and they have a point.[7]

All of this runs parallel with a deep skepticism and disinterest in democracy. Donald Trump was elected president by just 26.3 percent of eligible votes; almost 45 percent of voters didn't show up.[8] As we start to understand the moment we are living in, then slowly the work of the church starts to emerge. There is deep alienation; there is a desperation; there is a sense that nothing will ever work. Some express their fear by opting for a populist movement (whether Trump or Brexit); others are opting out. The symptoms (Trump or Brexit) are less interesting than the cause of the disease. Church should be confronting the cause, not simply moaning about the symptoms.

This read of our moment needs to invoke a basic wisdom. There are many ways healthcare can be developed. Some Christians might feel that private insurance will leave too many unable to get access to quality care and other Christians might hold the view that a national provider is both unaffordable and inefficient. There are many ways in which a tax system can be organized. Some Christians might support more redistribution than other Christians. As a Christian, I have views on all these things, but I am obligated to recognize that these are complex questions on which Christians can legitimately disagree. When it comes to policy disagreements among Christians, there must be a healthy and appropriate pluralism in a congregation. It is wrong for a rector to use the pulpit to advocate for this or that policy position. This is not the work of church.

There are, however, certain eternal imperatives that should always frame our preaching. The most important is the *Imago Dei*. Christians must consistently agree with and witness to this truth. All people are made in the Image of God. This is true of the immigrant, the Muslim, the Trump supporter, and the person with disabilities. This has signif-

---

7. Ibid., 162.
8. Ibid., 162–3.

icant implications. Racism is always completely wrong. If talk about immigration takes on certain generalizations about groups (for example, has racist characteristics), then it is wrong. It is, of course, possible to frame an immigration policy that avoids such generalizations. One could, for example, argue that open borders are impractical, therefore, some type of process of entry is essential, and that all forms of illegal immigration are wrong, and every effort should be made to stop such illegal immigration. Framed in this way, the position becomes a legitimate policy position that a Christian could hold.

Having touched on immigration, it is important to note that part of our moment is the reassertion of national identity. One offspring of globalization is the mobility of labor. People are on the move. Some are refugees fleeing a war zone or a place feeling the effects of climate change and others are in search of a better life. There is a backlash against the mobility of labor. People are feeling like strangers in neighborhoods that they have lived in all their lives. This has led to the reassertion of national identity. This is undoubtedly the case in respect to Brexit. Some voted to leave the European Union because they want to reassert their British (perhaps rather more often English) identity. So, this now leads to the second step: how should the preacher handle the deep emotional ties that people have to place?

The Deep Emotional Ties

The preacher must engage the reassertion of national identity. Some people want the world around them to be familiar; they want to be in a similar cultural setting and to have neighbors who share their values. They don't want their country to change. Often this is a mixture of patriotism and nostalgia.

Sociologically, this is complex. It often looks like America divides into countless value subgroups. Greenwich Village, in Lower Manhattan, is diverse, in terms of Asian Americans, African Americans, Hispanics, all mingling with Anglo-Americans, but the community shares a set of values that is pro-gay, very secular, supportive of globalization, and anti-Republican. Meanwhile Mesa, Arizona, ranked by Forbes as the most conservative city in the nation, shares a set of ideals that tend to support traditional values, like a belief in the importance of faith and the rule of law. It appears that like tends to gravitate to like.

Theologically, the question of patriotism is complex. To what extent is a Christian allowed to search out an environment where she or he is surrounded by like persons? To what extent is the Christian American allowed to aspire to keep the country "Christian"? To what extent can a Christian believe that America is by God's providence the best country in the world?

The temptation for some Christians is to dismiss nationalism, or even patriotism, as anti-Christian or to insist that love of country can never be uncritical and must include appropriate critique. Michael Long and Tracy Wenger Sadd write, "While politicians have raised their flags and demanded that we follow their version of American patriotism, many Christians have remained sheltered under steeples and ensconced in offices and pulpits."[9] They go on to call "for Christians to rethink U.S. patriotism on our own terms . . . ." Uncomplicated love of country is, for them, deeply problematic.[10]

The issue is complex. As a sociological reality, we must recognize the depth and passion of cultural identity with place. For a preacher to ignore this truth is to wade into deeply treacherous and volatile waters. Some identification with place and culture is appropriate. Home is where a family is. Home is where neighbors have formed deep bonds. Such connections are natural and healthy; indeed, they are part of the joy of living. It is wrong to say that such connections are wrong. Family ties are good and healthy. I have an obligation to care for my son differently than I have to care for other people's sons. My attachment to my son is intense in a way that I don't have for other people's sons. However—and this is an important however—the Christian ethic insists that my love for my son cannot exclude a love for and a care for other people's sons. Our sense of local identity should not be defined in such a way that it denigrates the identity of others. One's own sense of attachment to a child should create an empathy with other parents. I will do everything permissible to enable my son to survive and thrive and, therefore, it is not surprising that this is true of other parents. The

9. Michael G. Long and Tracy Wenger Sadd, "Introduction" in Michael G. Long and Tracy Wenger Sadd, *God and Country? Diverse Perspectives on Christianity and Patriotism* (New York: Palgrave Macmillan, 2007), 5.

10. Ibid.

refugee parents walking hundreds of miles to protect their children from gangs are simply living out their own sense of attachment to their children.

An historical perspective can be helpful here. Neighborhoods are always changing. From the vantage point of history, there was a time when America did not observe St. Patrick's Day and Irish neighborhoods did not exist. There was a time when the only inhabitants of America were Native Americans. People have been moving around the globe since the beginning. Cities, towns, and neighborhoods are constantly changing.

It is true that globalization has accelerated the process of the movement of people. Changes to a neighborhood that used to take decades can now happen in one year. Therefore, the preacher needs to be appropriately nuanced. First, the preacher should invite all Christians to recognize and celebrate their senses of attachment. The joy that family and friends bring to a life is good. The sense of belonging to a remarkable nation can be good. There is nothing sinful in these senses of attachment. Second, the preacher should invite all Christians to universalize those senses of attachment. All parents, save perhaps for a depraved or deeply damaged minority, have a deep love for their children. When an environment becomes unsafe, it is appropriate for the parents to want to keep their children safe. A sense of empathy is a Christian virtue. Third, Christians have an obligation to ensure that we witness to the intrinsic value of all people.

Preaching to the Underlying Anxieties of Our Time

If we are required as preachers to complexify our patriotism in light of the gospel, then we can start to see the key and underlying feature of preaching about politics. Our task is not to share our political prejudices with the congregation, but to locate our political dispositions within the perspective of eternity, grounded in the gospel.

When we read our historic moment (and, as I've suggested, Bremmer is a helpful commentator), we see that we are living in an age of acute anxiety. There is deep fear grounded in a lack of confidence about the positive benefits of globalization. There is a fear that "we" are becoming a minority, whether the English in Brexit, or the white fear of Mexicans taking over. The work of the gospel is to bring the presence of God to that fear.

"There is no fear in love, but perfect love casts out fear,"[11] writes the author of 1 John. We need to tap into the resources of the Gospel. There is a God. God is the creator of absolutely everything that is. God really does love us. There is nothing that can change that. Nothing from the divine perspective, not even death, can happen to us that can separate us "from the love of God in Christ Jesus our Lord" (Rom. 8:39).

The task of the preacher is to ignore the ephemeral nature of the immediate and tap into the deep fears of the human psyche. Racism is grounded in fear. Anxiety about globalization is grounded in fear. The populist movement has formed as an answer to that fear. One flirts with white supremacy because one is afraid that white people are disappearing under a demographic wave of persons of color. The gospel has the answer to such fears. We need to believe that God is, that God loves us, and that ultimately God will take care of us. It is that simple.

In Matthew 6, Jesus, speaking to an oppressed people who are under the occupation of the Romans, addresses "worry" head on. The people had much to worry about. It was an unstable time. Their neighborhoods were changing. The Romans were in charge. The potential for violence was ever present. And Jesus says,

Therefore I tell you, do not worry about your life, what you will eat or what you will drink, or about your body, what you will wear. Is not life more than food, and the body more than clothing? Look at the birds of the air; they neither sow nor reap nor gather into barns, and yet your heavenly Father feeds them. Are you not of more value than they? And can any of you by worrying add a single hour to your span of life? And why do you worry about clothing? Consider the lilies of the field, how they grow; they neither toil nor spin, yet I tell you, even Solomon in all his glory was not clothed like one of these. But if God so clothes the grass

---

11. 1 John 4:18. The actual context is the fear of punishment. When we abide in the love of God, we can be confident that God's love will not lead to punishment. However, the author does link it to the treatment of the brother and sister in Christ. Therefore, there is a sense in which love does displace fear more generally.

*of the field, which is alive today and tomorrow is thrown into the oven,
will he not much more clothe you—you of little faith? Therefore do not
worry, saying, 'What will we eat?' or 'What will we drink?' or 'What will
we wear?' For it is the Gentiles who strive for all these things; and indeed
your heavenly Father knows that you need all these things. But strive first
for the kingdom of God and his righteousness, and all these things will
be given to you as well. So do not worry about tomorrow, for tomorrow
will bring worries of its own. Today's trouble is enough for today*
(Matt. 6:25–34).

In my judgment, this is the most important text for the moment in
which we live. Anxiety generates fear. Fear generates a propensity
to believe in conspiracy theories (the Jews or the immigrants are the
problem). Once into the world of conspiracy theories, one is likely to
opt for extremist political solutions. Jesus addressed the problem of
anxiety head on.

It is an interesting text. The basic insight is that anxiety is a way
of destroying the gift of the moment we are living. Worry is not con-
structive. It is often predicated on a hypothetical that does not come
to pass. When one worries, one spoils the moment. Then the theme of
"trust" moves to the center. Given that God takes care of lilies, humans
are even more able to trust that ultimately God provides. Then comes
the promise that if we "strive first for the kingdom of God . . . all these
things will be given" to us. The conclusion of the text is the promise
that if we live out the reality of the kingdom, we are in a community
that will support us through the difficult times.

The stages of the argument are important for our moment. The
psychological stage is the futility of worry; the theological stage is the
imperative of trust of God; the ecclesiological stage is the centrality of
the community of the kingdom to provide the resources to enable us
to cope. In short, we need to turn every worry into a prayer, trust that
God is and will be there for us, and live into the reality of the kingdom
of mutual support.

This extended discussion of Matthew 6 makes a simple, basic point.
The work of church is to place our immediate concerns within the
context of eternity. It is to remind people that their companion on the
journey of life is the Creator of the universe. It is to stress that being

part of the church (the anticipation of the kingdom here now) means that you are part of a supportive community that will be there for you.

The challenge of our time is that we are flirting with extremist politics born out of economic frustration, a fear that globalization is not helping families to succeed, and a sense that change is happening at a disruptive speed. When church invites every single person to turn each of these anxieties into prayer, we are tackling the underlying issues that provoke the extremist politics.

It is at this fundamental level of human anxiety that church can work best. When we preach a gospel that God is, God loves, and that all our worries should be offered to God in prayer, the underlying anxieties of our lives are provided with a healthy outlet. The release is God instead of extremist politics.

Instead of the prophetic sermon that advocates for a political prescription that alienates half of the congregation, the preaching here confronts the underlying issues that can become politically destructive dispositions. It is prophetic preaching without being a sermon with an explicit political theme.

Eternal Significance and Prophetic Moment

It is tempting to finish this chapter on this theme: real prophetic preaching rarely touches on contemporary politics explicitly; but that would not be right. There are moments when a preacher needs to confront a political issue from the pulpit. If there is clear evidence of an unacceptable acceptance of anti-Semitism, then the preacher should name it. If there is evidence of growing racism, then it is entirely appropriate for the preacher to speak about it. However, it must be major and acute, comparable with the civil rights era.

The key doctrine is the *Imago Dei.* Of course, citizens are allowed to be concerned about terrorism, but Christians are not permitted to ascribe to generalizations that imply all Muslims are evil. Of course, citizens are allowed to be concerned about open borders, but Christians should never lose sight that the refugee is also a person loved by God.

This type of explicit political preaching will be rare. It needs to be an issue that rises to the level of eternal significance. Such preaching should recognize a legitimate pluralism, and the line drawn should be one that transcends left and right. The goal is always to the gospel, for the gospel advocates for the dignity of all people; the gospel alleviates anxiety; and the gospel creates a church that can support us all through the hard moments of life. This is the gift of prophetic preaching.

BIBLIOGRAPHY

Allen Jr., O. Wesley. *Preaching in the Era of Trump*. St. Louis, MO: Chalice Press, 2017.

Bremmer, Ian. *Us Vs. Them: The Failure of Globalism*. London: Portfolio Penguin, 2018.

Long, Michael G. and Tracy Wenger Sadd. "Introduction." In Michael G. Long and Tracy Wenger Sadd. *God and Country? Diverse Perspectives on Christianity and Patriotism*. New York: Palgrave Macmillan, 2007.

Marsh, Charles. *God's Long Summer*. Princeton, NJ: Princeton University Press, 1997.

Chapter 8

Prophetic Preaching as Sacrament
Finding and Using a Political Voice
Ruthanna Hooke

Political Preaching in These Times

The lead article in a recent issue of the *Christian Century* was entitled, "Do Politics Belong in Church?"[1] The article consisted of responses from pastors and theologians, most of whom concluded that the Christian faith cannot be divorced from the public and political spheres. As one writer put it, "Jesus Christ is Lord of *all* of life, including our political life."[2] Not to talk about politics in church is to suggest that believers can compartmentalize their lives, reserving our faith for the private sphere, and leaving public life to be ruled by other ideologies than Christian faith. Other writers point out that the Christian faith is eschatologically oriented toward the promise of God's reign coming on earth; the church's task is to bear witness to this inbreaking realm and to resist anything that stands against it. "I wouldn't be doing my job," wrote one pastor, "had I not mentioned Charlottesville the weekend after Heather Heyer was killed by white nationalists in 2017. Can we call ourselves followers of the Prince of Peace and not condemn violence born of bigotry and hate? Likewise, I don't see how we can read the story of Jesus welcoming the children and not have something

---

1. "Do Politics Belong in Church?," *Christian Century*, October 10, 2018, 20–26.
2. Scott Anderson, "Do Politics Belong in Church?," *Christian Century*, October 10, 2018, 23.

to say about the migrant children separated from their parents at the southern border."[3]

The reign of God brings about justice in history, and Christians are called to bear witness to this reign; thus, it is not only impossible to separate the religious from the political but dangerously self-deceptive to claim to do so. Stanley Hauerwas points out that the statement "religion and politics don't mix" is itself a political statement, and to refuse to take a political stand is to take a political stand, one that supports the status quo and those who benefit from it. "The illusion of being nonpolitical is a luxury of privilege that only leaves the vulnerable exposed," says James K.A. Smith.[4]

The question, then, is not *whether* preachers need to preach politically, but *how* to do so. It is an increasingly acute question in our current cultural context, in part because of our political climate, which is so polarized that much public speech cannot be heard outside of the speaker's echo chamber of like-minded people. It is increasingly difficult to hear each other across political differences because the basis of our public trust has been so compromised. In this environment, even words like "kindness" become suspect. The political has been taken over by the partisan. In addition, public speech has become so corrupted by falsehood, with accusations of "fake news" and claims to "alternative facts," that speech itself falls under suspicion. This poisoning infects preaching as well; by virtue of being public speech, it is suspected of being false.

In addition, deeper cultural forces make political preaching difficult. One of the few writers in *Christian Century* who did not advocate political preaching said that in her congregation, "Most people are looking for a respite from the barrage of ugly and disturbing news . . . They simply want something different, an opportunity that might offer a balm to their weary souls."[5] This soul-weariness is caused in

---

3. Lee Hull Moses, "Do Politics Belong in Church?," *Christian Century*, October 10, 2018, 20.

4. Stanley Hauerwas, "Do Politics Belong in Church?," *Christian Century,* October 10, 2018, 23; James K.A. Smith, "Do Politics Belong in Church?," *Christian Century*, October 10, 2018, 21.

5. Susan M. Reisart, "Do Politics Belong in Church?," *Christian Century*, October 10, 2018, 21.

part by the polarization and corruption of our public life, but this exhaustion has economic causes as well, as Kathryn Tanner's analysis of finance-dominated capitalism suggests. In finance capitalism, wealth is determined primarily not through the production of goods and service, but through schemes that maximize profit in the financial markets.[6] This system dominates our economic life and produces various pernicious effects: the work ethic is intensified, and people are considered morally culpable if they fail to meet its demands; responsibility for one's success or failure rests solely with the individual, with no help for those who make mistakes in their economic decisions; and the system fosters a highly competitive relationship with others. Most damagingly, this financial system is totalizing: "There is no 'you' apart from it; it covers the entirety of life, at work and outside of it, and the whole of one's aspirations, in the way, for instance, that being indebted colonizes one's past, present, and future."[7] Finance capitalism makes it impossible to imagine any escape from the current economic order. The upshot of such a system is a deformation of human beings and their communities. Bruce Rogers-Vaughn argues that in neoliberal capitalism humans exhibit what he calls "third-order suffering," in which the human subject becomes fragmented, isolated, and separated from institutions and traditions. Third-order suffering is "suffering that is not aware of itself as suffering."[8] It may manifest itself as depression, addiction, or a tendency to blame oneself for this diffuse misery for which there seems to be no one else to blame.[9] Overall, the totalizing regime of global capitalism withers the soul—soul being "an aspect of the embodied self, namely *the activity of self-transcendence* . . . that activity which holds individuals in relation with self, others, creation, and the Eternal."[10] Ian Markham, in his essay in this volume, likewise points to the negative effects of global capitalism on the working class in the United States, which has caused a sense

6. Kathryn Tanner, *Christianity and the New Spirit of Capitalism* (New Haven: Yale University Press, 2019).

7. Ibid., 28

8. Bruce Rogers-Vaughn, *Caring for Souls in a Neoliberal Age* (New York: Palgrave Macmillan, 2016), 169.

9. Ibid., 126.

10. Ibid., 5.

of alienation and desperation that belies the supposed triumphs of globalization.

Homiletician Charles Campbell describes such circumstances as captivity to the powers and principalities, spiritual forces that are active in our institutions and systems. We are in the grip of these powers of death, such that "we are no longer agents of our own lives, but go through the deadly motions dictated to us by the powers of the world that hold us captive."[11] For instance, we are told that consumption is salutary and so we consume addictively, even though it is destroying our planet and entails the suffering of those who produce the commodities we consume. Or we are told that technology will give us convenience and freedom, whereas we find ourselves captive to our devices, which fragment our attention and separate us from others and even our own sense of self.[12] When looking at the overwhelming problems of our world, such as the current climate crisis, people become paralyzed and feel powerless to change anything. Campbell notes that preachers face "not so much evil minds as paralyzed consciences. The problem is not so much malevolence as the *de*moralization of people 'who have become captive and immobilized as human beings by their habitual obeisance to institutions or other principalities as idols.'"[13] Preachers do not face people who actively desire evil, but rather people who are trapped in dehumanizing systems in which they themselves are complicit, and that seem to have eternal sway over our lives. It is not surprising that souls are weary when they come to church, and may long for respite in preaching, rather than political challenge.

These diagnoses of the contemporary human condition compel preachers to rethink how we preach politically. Preachers need to reclaim specifically Christian understandings of both political preach-

---

11. Charles L. Campbell, "Resisting the Powers," in *Purposes of Preaching*, ed. Jana Childers (St. Louis: Chalice Press, 2004), 27.

12. See, *inter alia*, Sherry Turkle, *Alone Together: Why We Expect More from Technology and Less from Each Other* (New York: Basic Books, 2011) and Andrew Sullivan, "I Used to be a Human Being," in *New York*, September 19, 2016, http://nymag.com/intelligencer/2016/09/andrew-sullivan-my-distraction-sickness-and-yours.html.

13. Campbell, "Resisting the Powers," 28. Quote is from William Stringfellow, *An Ethic for Christians and Other Aliens in a Strange Land,* 3rd edition (Waco, TX: Word Books, 1979), 29–30.

ing and of politics itself. As Stanley Hauerwas notes, "What is essential is . . . to avoid letting what passes as politics determine the political agenda of the church. Christians must learn again how to reframe issues in a manner that makes clear that the politics of Jesus is different."[14] Hauerwas points out that "'Issues' are what politicians use to distract 'the people' from considering the fundamental injustices of our political arrangements."[15] The church's preaching needs to address deeper political realities, such as those described by Tanner, Campbell, Markham, and others, rather than the "issues" that dominate the news cycle. It is crucial that the church's *mode* of political speech be different from the modes of speech of the surrounding culture. There is a desperate need for public speech that is political without being partisan, truthful as well as loving, and that can reach us in our soul-weary captivity to the powers.

The Political, the Prophetic, and the Sacramental

Two strands of the Anglican preaching tradition offer promise in providing models of political preaching: preaching as prophetic and preaching as sacramental. These two strands of the tradition are often opposed to each other, in the supposed opposition of the priestly and the prophetic, but I will argue that a meeting of the prophetic and the sacramental yields a particularly Anglican model of political preaching that can address our current circumstances effectively.

Although, as Sarah Condon notes in chapter two, preachers can claim the mantle of the prophet for grandiose or self-seeking reasons, the prophetic strand of the Judeo-Christian tradition is nevertheless a rich resource for developing a uniquely Christian mode of political speech. Although "political" and "prophetic" preaching are often used interchangeably, the prophetic is a richer term than the political, more rooted in our tradition, and offering understandings of preaching that are more hearable in these times. John McClure defines prophetic preaching as "an imaginative reappropriation of traditional narratives and symbols for the purpose of critiquing a dangerous and unjust present situation

---

14. Hauerwas, *Christian Century*, 23.
15. Ibid.

and providing an alternative vision of God's future."[16] This definition emphasizes that the prophet stands within the tradition, drawing from its authority to critique the present. The Hebrew prophets were deeply conservative, calling Israel back to its covenant with God. McClure's definition also draws on Walter Brueggemann's description of the two registers in which prophets speak: they unmask and lament the current order, and they also energize the people by providing a vision of hope. Like Hauerwas, Brueggemann redefines the political by insisting that the prophet's task is to nurture a consciousness alternative to that of the dominant culture: "Prophetic ministry has to do not primarily with addressing specific public crises but with addressing . . . the dominant crisis that is enduring and resilient, of having our alternative vocation coopted and domesticated."[17]

In exercising their ministry, prophets speak *from within* their community, not *over and against* it. This is particularly important, as Campbell points out, when preaching to people who are captive to the powers and principalities. The tone of preaching needs to be compassionate and upbuilding, rather than judgmental, since all are captives, including the preacher. Judgment is directed toward unjust circumstances and systems where the powers are operative, rather than toward individuals.[18] It is a misconception, therefore, to set the prophetic over against the priestly and pastoral. The prophetic role is deeply pastoral, since it is a ministry to people in their captivity to evils from which they long to be set free. Moreover, it is the prophet's love for the people that causes their anguish when present situations contradict God's purposes.

Prophets are defined by their intimate relationship to God. Abraham Heschel, in his classic work on the Hebrew prophets, states that "the fundamental experience of the prophet is a fellowship with the feelings of God, *a sympathy with the divine pathos.*"[19] The prophet dares

16. John McClure, *Preaching Words: 144 Key Terms in Homiletics* (Louisville, KY: Westminster John Knox Press, 2007), 117.

17. Walter Brueggemann, *The Prophetic Imagination*, 2nd edition (Minneapolis: Fortress Press, 2001), 3.

18. Charles L. Campbell, *The Word Before the Powers: An Ethic of Preaching* (Louisville, KY: Westminster John Knox Press, 2002), 149.

19. Abraham Heschel, *The Prophets: An Introduction*, vol. 1 (New York: Harper & Row, 1962), 26.

to say, "Thus says the Lord," to speak on God's behalf, because he participates in God's life, shares God's agony over those things that contradict God's reign, and perceives God's vision for this world. Leonora Tubbs Tisdale claims that prophetic preaching "requires of the preacher a heart that breaks with the things that break God's heart," and "the imagination, conviction and courage to speak words from God."[20]

Anglican preaching can reclaim this prophetic preaching tradition by bringing a sacramental emphasis to it. Among the most notable qualities of Anglican/Episcopal preaching is that it is liturgical, usually taking place in conjunction with the Eucharist. Word and sacrament are balanced in a relationship of equality that few other branches of the Christian tradition sustain as fully. For Anglicans, preaching and Eucharist are a counterpoint to each other; each are doing the same thing in a different way, in that each is a means of encountering God. The Eucharist is, therefore, a form of proclamation, and preaching is sacramental. I propose that preaching understood sacramentally can be prophetic and hence political in ways that are uniquely appropriate to our current cultural circumstances. In the remainder of this essay I will outline four aspects of the preaching event, which parallel four aspects of the Eucharist. Just as the celebration of the Eucharist is a material, embodied event, so too preaching is an embodied event, whose meaning is rooted in the bodies of both preacher and hearers. Thus, I will argue that each of these aspects of preaching can be experienced in the body and voice of preacher and hearers. As preaching inhabits each of these dimensions of sacramental preaching, it can offer a prophetic message that can be received in these times.

The Real Presence of the Preacher

However they describe the transformation that takes place in the elements of the Eucharist, Anglicans tend to believe in the "real presence" of Christ in the Eucharist. The Eucharist is not a mere memorial of Christ's death and resurrection, but an encounter with his living presence. The parallel claim made by Luther and others is that the sermon, too, is an event in which God is really present. This "high" view of

---

20. Leonora Tubbs Tisdale, *Prophetic Preaching: A Pastoral Approach* (Louisville, KY: Westminster John Knox, 2010), 10.

preaching need not lead to a "high" view of the preacher. Karl Barth, who insists that preaching is the Word of God no less than scripture and Jesus Christ, on whom the preached Word depends, argues that this exalted view of preaching actually requires the humility of the preacher, since the fact that preaching is the Word of God is entirely due to God's grace, rather than to anything inherent in the preacher.

In both the Eucharist and preaching, God's presence is mediated through materiality—in the Eucharist, through the bread and wine and, in preaching, through the preacher. Their body and voice, particularity and history, are the media through which the divine Word is made flesh. Although this event is a gift of grace, the preacher can make themselves available to it by the quality of their presence. This presence has three essential attributes: integration—the unity of body, mind, and soul; integrity—the coherence of one's words, action, and selfhood; and connectedness—to God and to the hearers. Fully embodied presence is inherently presence in relationship with others, because to be human is to be relational. We are created in the image of God, who is triune relationship in God's own being. We are created for the purpose of relationship with God, to be drawn into God's triune being of love, and to love our neighbor as the expression of this divine calling. To be present is to manifest this openness to God and neighbor.

For a preacher to be fully present requires a lifetime of disciplined growth in love and courage. Physical practices can assist in this becoming-present; they allow the body to be present, which creates the conditions for the soul and mind to be present as well, so that the speaker is integrated. These practices involve finding a stance of alignment, the skeleton supporting the body so that the body is standing with minimal effort and tension. The preacher can establish this presence in the moment of silence prior to the first word of the sermon, and can return to it as a touchstone throughout the sermon.

This moment of silence is sacramental, akin to the taking and offering the elements of bread and wine on the altar. It is also prophetic, in part in that it is a gesture of self-offering. Prophetic preaching is rooted in intimacy with God; the prophetic preacher offers themselves as a channel for God to speak. At the same time, in this moment of silence the preacher establishes a communion with their hearers, in effect saying to the congregation, "I am here with you, as together we await God's Word." Just as the Hebrew prophets spoke from within their communities, so too the prophetic preacher stands with their listeners under the Word.

This establishment of community between preacher and hearers is in itself prophetic and political. Both Tanner and Rogers-Vaughn focus on the building of communities as a remedy to the dehumanizing effects of neoliberal finance capitalism. Tanner writes that the most successful resistance to finance capitalism is "a community forged according to very different assumptions about how relations to one-self bear on relations with others."[21] The community is united not around financial dependence on each other, but rather dependence on God as the source and goal of life: "the very same object of love and knowledge is made the basis of a common vision and desire," drawing the community together in ways that overcome division and competition.[22] The existence of this community united in its desire for God demonstrates the existence of a world outside of capitalism, resisting its totalizing claims. Likewise, Rogers-Vaughn calls for resistance to neoliberal capitalism via collectives that nurture soul and amplify hope, countering the isolation of human beings which is a key marker of third-order suffering.[23] If communities are a form of political resistance, a central task of the political preacher is the strengthening of the community in which they preach. This can be done in forging the connection between preacher and hearers in the preaching event itself, beginning with the moment of silence preceding it. This moment is in itself political.

This moment of silence is also a time of simply resting in God's presence, signaling the gift of Sabbath rest, which is a political act. Tanner argues that the ideology of finance capitalism defines the value of humankind entirely by their work. Campbell notes that one way the powers maintain their hegemony is by keeping us ceaselessly busy,

---

21. Tanner, *Christianity and the New Spirit,* 210.
22. Ibid., 218.
23. Rogers-Vaughn, *Caring for Souls,* 211.

in part so that we are too exhausted even to see our captivity to those same powers. In such environments, enjoying Sabbath rest is an act of political resistance. It is a way of acknowledging that "running directly contrary to a work ethic, however, one's value in God's eyes is not *conditional* upon particular achievements that distinguish one from others . . . we are not responsible for creating the value of what we are and will be through productive activities."[24] Not only does the Sabbath acknowledge humans' value apart from their work, but it also acknowledges the sovereignty of God as greater than that of the powers that demand our worship. Furthermore, the Sabbath is a basis for ethics, because in pausing to listen for God we learn to be directed by God, rather than the chatter of the culture around us.

For these reasons, the Sabbath is one of the most *political* doctrines we can preach; it is an example of what Hauerwas calls the church's political agenda, which is different from the political issues of the day. Prophetic preachers are called upon not only to preach *about* the Sabbath, but also to *manifest* it in their preaching, and one way they can do this is to rest in silence even before the sermon begins. Silence can punctuate the sermon at various points, allowing for the experience of Sabbath to undergird the sermon in its entirety. Even if the hearers do not consciously grasp the meanings of these silences, the Holy Spirit communicates through these moments to shape the community according to the logic of God's reign.

The Preaching *Epiclesis*:
The Coming of the Holy Spirit

In the celebration of the Eucharist, the material elements that are present on the altar are made holy when the Holy Spirit comes upon them at the *epiclesis*. This moment echoes many events in scripture when the Spirit brought God's life, and paradigmatically the Spirit's overshadowing Mary, so that the Word became flesh and dwelt among us. Analogously, the Word is made flesh in the sermon when the Holy Spirit breathes within and between the preacher and the congregation. As Sarah Coakley notes, it is the Holy Spirit that draws us into the inner-trinitarian life of God; this inspiration of the sermon by the

---

24. Tanner, *Christianity and the New Spirit,* 208. Emphasis Tanner's.

Holy Spirit, like the *epiclesis* upon the elements in the Eucharist, is an instance of being drawn into the triune life of God.[25]

This is a process that can be felt physically, in the breathing of both preacher and listeners. In scripture, the Holy Spirit is consistently imagined as the *ruach*, the *pneuma*, the breath of God that brings life, from the Spirit moving over the face of the deep at the beginning of creation to the risen Jesus reviving the frightened disciples by breathing on them and saying, "Receive the Holy Spirit" (John 20:22). To unpack this metaphor by exploring the physical experience of breathing in relation to speaking points to the Holy Spirit's role in prophetic preaching.

The breath supports the voice; it is only by allowing breath into our bodies that we can speak with the fullness of our voice. Likewise, it is only through the in-spiration (the breathing into us) of the Holy Spirit that we are able to preach God's life-giving Word. The sermon is both a human and a divine action. The preacher brings their gifts and particular experience to the sermon, but it is only the life-giving Word made flesh when it is in-spired by the Holy Spirit. Moreover, breathing is a *passive* action; rather than making ourselves breathe, it is more accurate to say that we *are breathed*. This physical fact reminds us of Barth's insistence that God's being present with us in the sermon is a divine gift rather than a human attainment.

The Holy Spirit's breathing in us draws us closer to God's life, and into community with each other, creating "unity of the Spirit" (Eph. 4:3). The breath connects us to each other; the philosopher Emmanuel Levinas describes breathing as an opening of the self to the other: one "frees oneself by breathing from closure in oneself."[26] This connection to God and to other humans through the Holy Spirit allows us to participate in the "sufferings of this present time." We share creation's groaning in labor pains, since "we who have the first fruits of the Spirit groan inwardly while we wait for adoption, the redemption of our bodies." In this suffering the Spirit "helps us in our weakness . . .

---

25. Sarah Coakley, *God, Sexuality and the Self: An Essay 'On the Trinity'* (Cambridge: Cambridge University Press, 2013), 330.

26. Emmanuel Levinas, *Otherwise than Being or Beyond Essence*, trans. Alphonso Lingis (Pittsburgh, PA: Duquesne Press, 1998), 180.

interced[ing] with sighs too deep for words" (Rom. 8:26). To have the Holy Spirit is to labor with those who suffer and to feel the agony that God feels that this world is not yet as God intends it to be. It is allowing the Holy Spirit to pray within us, even with sighs that go beyond all words. This sympathy with the divine pathos is the essence of prophecy; to speak from this inspired compassion allows the preacher to pierce the numbness of third-order suffering that keeps hearers captive to the powers. Thus, this seemingly simple practice of breathing opens us to the divine agony and compassion that makes prophetic preaching possible.

The Holy Spirit breathing in us also awakens the courage to prophesy, since it is the Spirit who empowers prophetic utterance. In Jesus's first sermon, he declares: "The Spirit of the Lord is upon me, because he has anointed me to bring good news to the poor . . . " (Luke 4:18). That same Spirit descends upon the disciples at Pentecost, fulfilling Joel's prophecy: "In these last days it shall be, God declares, that I shall pour out my Spirit upon all flesh, and your sons and your daughters shall prophesy" (Acts 2:17). This prophecy signals the beginning of the prophetic mission of the earliest Christian disciples. The Spirit continues to empower this mission, such that when the disciples are hauled before rulers to testify to their faith, Jesus promises that "the Holy Spirit will teach you at that very hour what you ought to say" (Luke 12:11–12). Liturgical theologians describe the *epiclesis* in the Eucharistic prayer as a moment of "dangerous memory," in which the Spirit's coming upon the elements connects us both to the radical political challenge of Jesus's person and work, and also to the eschatological inbreaking of God's realm of justice.[27] Likewise, the *epiclesis* upon the preacher connects the sermon to God's prophetic Word preached in Jesus's person and work, as well as to the eschatological promise of God's just reign.

On a physical level, prophetic-sacramental preaching calls for the preacher to make his body available for *epiclesis*, for the coming of the Holy Spirit in the breath. This is surprisingly difficult to do. We often do not breathe freely; tension and fear frequently cause us to tighten

---

27. Bruce Morrill, *Anamnesis as Dangerous Memory* (Collegeville, MN: Liturgical Press, 2000), 185.

our breathing muscles to the point where we are only allowing a small amount of breath to enter, which means our voices are not fully supported. Perhaps our unwillingness to breathe fully is a resistance to the Spirit's presence, our reluctance to feel the depths of God's anguish or that of our neighbors, or our fear of accepting the Spirit's prophetic urging. In that case, overcoming this resistance can begin with as simple a practice as allowing breath into our bodies as we preach. To allow the Spirit to breathe in us is itself a political act, which may prompt us to follow Jesus in proclaiming good news to the poor and release to the captives, inspiring us to dream dreams, see visions, and testify before rulers, announcing God's realm of justice before the powers of this world.

The Breaking of the Word

The Spirit's coming upon the preacher draws them into God's triune life, uniting them to the Word made flesh. To preach this incarnate Word is to follow the trajectory of that Word in the death and resurrection of Jesus Christ. The Eucharist is a proclamation of the Lord's death (1 Cor. 11:26), symbolized in the breaking of the bread, which enacts the breaking of the Word upon the cross. Comparing preaching to the sacrament suggests that there is a breaking of the Word in the preaching event, as preaching manifests the way of the cross, both in the sermon's content and in how the preacher preaches.

Paul provides the paradigmatic example of what preaching looks like when it is completely shaped by the cross of Jesus Christ. The cross not only dictated the *content* of Paul's preaching, but also *how he preached*:

> When I came to you, brothers and sisters, I did not come proclaiming the mystery of God to you in lofty words or wisdom. For I decided to know nothing among you except Christ, and him crucified. And I came to you in much weakness and in fear and much trembling. My speech and my proclamation were not with plausible words and wisdom, but with a demonstration of the Spirit and of power, so that your faith might not rest upon human wisdom but on the power of God.
>
> *1 Cor. 2:1–5*

Paul's preaching takes on the quality of Christ crucified: it is folly and
weakness by human standards, so that God's power and wisdom might
become more apparent. His fear and trembling, and his own lack of
rhetorical polish, are precisely what allows the gospel of Jesus Christ to
be proclaimed. Paul is "always carrying in the body the death of Jesus,
so that the life of Jesus may be made visible in our bodies" (2 Cor. 4:7,
10). It is not so much what Paul *says* about Christ crucified as how he
manifests this doctrine in his entire life that proclaims its truth.

For preachers to carry in their bodies the death of Jesus, inhabiting
the sacramental breaking of the Word, would mean to proclaim the
ways in which Christ is still crucified in our political life. This unmask-
ing exposes the deathliness of royal consciousness, and proclaims an
end to it:

> The cross is the ultimate metaphor of prophetic criticism because it
> means the end of the old consciousness that brings death on every-
> one. The crucifixion articulates God's odd freedom, his strange jus-
> tice, and his peculiar power . . . that break[s] the power of the old age
> and bring[s] it to death.[28]

To preach Christ crucified is not only a matter of the content of one's
preaching, for to carry the cross of Christ in one's body also requires
a certain manner of preaching. As Brueggemann notes, "Without the
cross, prophetic imagination will likely be as strident and as destructive as that which it criticizes. The cross is the assurance that effective
prophetic criticism is done not by an outsider but always by one who
must embrace the grief, enter into the death, and know the pain of the
criticized one."[29]

To preach Christ crucified is to preach with *passion*, which means
to enter into Christ's passion, feeling in the body the sufferings and
injustices of which one speaks. Preaching Christ crucified entails a willingness to suffer alongside those who suffer; here the prophetic and
the priestly come together, since a priest is one who feels the people's
suffering and carries it to God. Preaching Christ crucified ultimately

---

28. Brueggemann, *The Prophetic Imagination*, 99.
29. Ibid., 99.

means a *kenosis* of the self, which allows the power of God to be that much more apparent. This act defies the powers and their "spirit of control," because it is giving control over to God, which may mean even giving up one's life as a witness/martyr. Such preaching passion can break through the numbness of our captivity to the powers, our third-order suffering.

Such radical self-donation is the work of a lifetime of prayer, but again there are physical practices that assist in speaking with this passion. These practices have to do with how we use our voices. We are created such that our voices belong to our entire bodies, rather than to the head alone, and our voices can reveal our selves—the full range of our thoughts, feelings, and impulses. We rarely experience our voices in this way, since the effects of social conditioning, trauma, and the stresses of everyday life cause us to disconnect our voices from our bodies and from the truths that our embodied souls know.[30] To preach Christ crucified, to preach with the passion of Christ, requires reconnecting our voices to our bodies' and souls' depths, to truths we know but are afraid to speak, so that communication is once again a fully embodied revelation of selfhood. This self-revelation is also a revelation of God, the becoming-flesh of God's Word through our own flesh. As our voices connect with our own depths, they also intrinsically connect us to God and to each other. This is so because, as made in the image of the triune God, we are relational beings; true speech reveals the communion that is always there. As Levinas observes, the true purpose of human speech is to signal our connection to each other, and this signaling precedes and underlies any particular content to our speaking.[31] Bruce Rogers-Vaughn notes that nurturing the soul is about speaking and listening: "Soul is a self-transcendence that occurs within dialogue, in the form of the call-and-response of relationship."[32] This communication breaks through the isolation that defines third-order suffering, a suffering that often entails a loss of

---

30. This analysis of the embodied voice is found in Kristin Linklater, *Freeing the Natural Voice: Imagery and Art in the Practice of Voice and Language*, revised and expanded edition (Hollywood, CA: Drama Publishers, 2006).

31. Levinas, *Otherwise than Being*, 143.

32. Rogers-Vaughn, *Caring for Souls*, 231.

both physical and metaphorical voice.[33] Such speaking is rooted in the compassion of Christ, and is open rather than self-protective, modeling a different mode of speech from the defensive and fear-based rhetoric so common in our public life.

The Sharing of the Word

The final stage of the Eucharist is the sharing of the body of Christ, the communion itself. In this moment the congregation receives the body of Christ, bringing them into union with God and with each other, reminding them that they *are* the body of Christ. The community formed in the liturgy is now commissioned to bring Christ's body into the world. The Eucharist is one of the principal ways that Christians become a community dedicated to living differently than the world around them. William Cavanaugh describes the formational power of the Eucharist in *Torture and Eucharist,* in which he analyzes the Chilean Roman Catholic Church's resistance to dictatorship, arguing that the Eucharist became the primary way that the church formed a community capable of resisting the imagination of the state.[34] The Eucharist can form communities of what Brueggemann calls "alternative consciousness" capable of nurturing the prophetic imagination. Campbell proposes that forming communities committed to Christian practices is the most effective way of resisting the powers.[35]

Like the Eucharist, preaching forms and commissions the hearers to live as bearers of the Word, presenting an alternative vision for how life can be lived according to God's purposes. This is a crucial aspect of the prophetic vocation: the preacher not only proclaims Christ crucified by critiquing the order that resists God's realm, but proclaims a vision of hope for this coming reign, grounded in Christ's resurrection. Here again, though, what is important is not only *what* the preacher says, but *how* she says it, how she manifests the power of the resurrection.

Physically, this power is suggested by the power of the voice, in

---

33. Ibid.

34. William T. Cavanaugh, *Torture and Eucharist: Theology, Politics, and the Body of Christ* (Oxford: Blackwell Publishers, 1998), 206.

35. Campbell, *The Word Before the Powers*, 129 ff.

which extra breath power is harnessed and all the resonators in the body are awakened, so that the voice has its full range and freedom. Speaking with the free voice is not meant to glorify the preacher, but to awaken the community's own power. Just as the body of Christ in the Eucharist is given to the congregation to remind them that they *are* the body of Christ, called to be his body in the world, in preaching the Word is given to the congregation so that they can claim their own vocation as proclaimers of the Word. The preacher's speech and presence iconically demonstrates to hearers how they too can claim the task of prophetic proclamation.

This means that prophetic preaching must be rooted in love, from the initial moment of silence to the most powerful heights of speaking. Paul begins 1 Corinthians by describing his preaching of Christ crucified; he ends the letter by proclaiming the resurrection. However, just before describing this mystery, he comes back to preaching, and here his emphasis falls on love as the *sine qua non* of prophetic speech: "If I speak with the tongues of mortals and of angels, but have not love, I am a noisy gong or a clanging cymbal" (1 Cor. 13:1, 5). The route that goes from crucifixion to resurrection is the way of love. Love is the touchstone for preaching that is sacramental, as well as the foundation and end of prophetic proclamation.

Conclusion

A sacramental description of prophetic preaching focuses above all on the *way* that preaching is carried out, as much as on the content of the proclamation. For prophetic preaching to be hearable in these soul-weary times, it is vital that the preacher forge a deeper and truer connection with God, themselves, and their congregation. This deeper connection needs to be made not only in the soul but in the body. Learning how to be present, how to let the Spirit's breath into the body, how to connect one's voice to one's depths and to allow that voice to come forth in power and love, are physical practices that can support preaching that is prophetic, priestly, and pastoral. Above all, it is rooted in love, the costly love of Jesus's death and resurrection. This is a love that can commission Christian communities to offer a prophetic and political witness that can be heard in these times.

BIBLIOGRAPHY

Brueggemann, Walter. *The Prophetic Imagination*. 2nd Edition. Minneapolis: Fortress Press, 2001.

Campbell, Charles L. "Resisting the Powers." In *Purposes of Preaching*, edited by Jana Childers, 23–28. St. Louis: Chalice Press, 2004.

Campbell, Charles L. *The Word Before the Powers: An Ethic of Preaching*. Louisville, KY: Westminster John Knox Press, 2002.

Cavanaugh, William T. *Torture and Eucharist: Theology, Politics, and the Body of Christ*. Oxford: Blackwell Publishers, 1998.

Coakley, Sarah. *God, Sexuality and the Self: An Essay 'On the Trinity.'* Cambridge: Cambridge University Press, 2013.

"Do Politics Belong in Church?" *Christian Century*. October 10, 2018.

Heschel, Abraham. *The Prophets: An Introduction*. Vol. 1. New York: Harper & Row, 1962.

Levinas, Emmanuel. *Otherwise than Being or Beyond Essence*. Translated by Alphonso Lingis. Pittsburgh, PA: Duquesne Press, 1998.

Linklater, Kristin. *Freeing the Natural Voice: Imagery and Art in the Practice of Voice and Language*. Revised and expanded edition. Hollywood, CA: Drama Publishers, 2006.

McClure, John. *Preaching Words: 144 Key Terms in Homiletics*. Louisville, KY: Westminster John Knox Press, 2007.

Morrill, Bruce. *Anamnesis as Dangerous Memory*. Collegeville, Minneapolis: Liturgical Press, 2000.

Rogers-Vaughn, Bruce. *Caring for Souls in a Neoliberal Age*. New York: Palgrave Macmillan, 2016.

Sullivan, Andrew. "I Used to be a Human Being." In *New York*, September 19, 2016. http://nymag.com/intelligencer/2016/09/andrew-sullivan-my-distraction-sickness-and-yours.html.

Tanner, Kathryn. *Christianity and the New Spirit of Capitalism*. New Haven: Yale University Press, 2019.

Tisdale, Leonora Tubbs. *Prophetic Preaching: A Pastoral Approach*. Louisville, KY: Westminster John Knox, 2010.

Turkle, Sherry. *Alone Together: Why We Expect More from Technology and Less from Each Other*. New York: Basic Books, 2011.

Chapter 9

Getting the Basics Right

Samuel Wells

I have two kinds of sermons. The first I call exegetical and the second I call pastoral. When I prepare the first, I am captivated by a passage of scripture, which is almost always one of the set readings for the day, or given to me by the occasion or the person inviting me—it's almost never of my own choosing. I'm not always struck straightaway, but as I ponder, examine, and read about that passage, either the structure, the terminology, or the argument strikes me. Sometimes just one phrase or sentence jumps out. Thereafter, I seek to identify what is so special about that passage, sentence, or phrase, and I prepare a sermon crafted to arouse in the congregation a thirst to wrestle with a conundrum or resolve a quandary to which that passage, sentence, or phrase is an answer or a resolution. I almost never start with the passage, sentence, or phrase itself; that would be like blurting out the punch line before you tell the joke. I don't usually introduce the passage in question until the congregation is already eager to resolve a tension that my opening remarks have identified. It may not be a tension the listener was aware of before, but in a few sentences I seek to make the listener aware of it so acutely that they are on tenterhooks to know what the resolution will be. The sermon is satisfying to the extent that the attention and expectation aroused is in keeping with, and on a theme identical with, the resolution the exposition of the passage, sentence, or phrase provides. Most satisfying of all is being able to return to an insignificant element of the material with which I began and show, at the end, that it has an even greater significance than was previously disclosed. Ideally that will be a Christological dimension that was abiding in the passage but had not been apparent until that point.

The second kind of sermon doesn't begin with a scriptural passage. It begins with a question in the hearts and minds of the congregation. It may be that something significant has come to pass in the congregation's life, planned or accidental: perhaps Giving Sunday, in the former case; a family tragedy in the latter. It may be that a major event has taken place in the national or global domain, anticipated or sudden: the hosting of the Olympic Games, perhaps, or the death of a noted politician. It may be that the church, locally or denominationally, is consumed with a pressing theological or ethical question. It may be that the wider culture is wrestling with a question that is so timely it simply demands homiletical engagement. Or it may be that there is a question the wider church and culture are not actively discussing that I sincerely believe they should be, and I wish to put forward some framework for the conversation. The way I do this is rather different from the first approach. I usually start with a theological insight. It may be from church history or from a classic theological controversy. Sometimes it will be a careful procedural move, like the methods of over-accepting and reincorporation I discuss at some length in my own writing.[1] I then ponder where in the scriptures that insight is most aptly expressed. In almost every case the passage I arrive at has more interesting things to say than just the part I was thinking of, and so I pause to explore how there is more to say from this part of scripture than I originally imagined. Then I construct an argument based in most cases on an attempt at an even-handed overview of the issue, a move that draws in the existential and emotional depth and range of the question, and a recognition of where the pressure points lie. From this point on, the two kinds of sermons are broadly similar, even though they have emerged from different thought-processes and serve different purposes. If I am seeking to address a pastoral issue on a Sunday morning, I shall almost always seek to do so from one of the texts set for the day. The only exception might be in the event of a major unexpected congregational or global crisis such as 9/11 or the sudden death of a very visible member of the community.

---

1. Samuel Wells, *Improvisation: The Drama of Christian Ethics,* 2nd edition (Grand Rapids: Baker, 2018).

So-called prophetic sermons fall almost entirely into the second kind—occasions when a pastoral need makes it necessary or unavoidable to tread on contested ground, within church or world or both. If people like what we are saying they may call it prophetic; if not, they may call it misguided, unwise, inappropriate, taking advantage, imposing your convictions, or venting. I want now to offer an example of this more edgy kind of pastoral sermon and to provide a commentary on it, before summarizing my suggestions. My hope is that the reader, if the reader is also a preacher, may find that if they preach an edgy pastoral sermon and face criticism, they may then, if they follow the guidelines I offer, recognize the costs of ministry. If they don't follow the guidelines, they may acknowledge that they might have got it wrong this time.

The following sermon I preached twice on the same day. In the evening, I was explicitly asked to speak on the subject of Brexit for a service at a Cambridge college, as part of an eight-part series entitled "Christian Engagement with Public Debates." Somewhat lazily, I noticed that Revelation 21 was among the assigned readings for the morning service at my own church, and I decided to preach a longer version of the same sermon that morning. What follows is the longer version.

Discovering Who We Are
Revelation 21
A sermon preached at St. Martin-in-the-Fields
on November 4, 2018

Two years ago in the Brexit referendum this country was divided between leavers and remainers. In truth few remainers believed the European Union was the fount of every blessing, while few leavers really thought Britain would finally realize its eternal destiny the moment it left the EU. Instead, for both sides, the issue of whether or not to remain in the EU became a touchstone about other issues closer to people's hearts, about multiculturalism, democracy, belonging, and rapid social change. I want today to take a step back from the intensity of chaos and controversy and explore what this is really all about.

Let's start with a story that I hope is relatively uncontroversial. After the hangover of VE Day and VJ Day, Britain woke up in 1945 to find itself in a different world. The United States now sat at the head of the table, Russia glowered at it from the far end, the empire was disintegrating, Europe was half destroyed, and a way had to be found to restore Germany without it yet again finding itself at war with France and Russia. For a long period it looked like the answer to almost all these questions was the European Union. Yet underlying the European Union was a vision to which Britain never adhered, a vision of full economic and eventual political union. After nearly twenty years of trying, Britain joined the EEC in 1973, but crucially Edward Heath made the case on economic grounds rather than on questions of identity.

Britain continued to see its identity largely elsewhere—as a Security Council member, in the so-called "special relationship" with the United States, amongst the Commonwealth. Whenever critical questions of economic and political union surfaced, Britain always dragged its feet. The habit of assuming we could take the parts of Europe we wanted was most evident in the refusal to join the single currency. You may know the story of the silent monastery. After ten years a monk was invited to his first audience with the abbot and was granted two words. He said: "Food cold." Ten years later he was granted his second audience and was allowed two more words: "Room cold." After thirty years the monk was granted his third audience, and announced, "I'm leaving." "Good riddance," the abbot replied, "you've done nothing but complain ever since you've been here." That's been the story of Britain in Europe these last forty-five years.

There's always been a simmering discontent within Britain about membership of the European Union. Some of that has been political: many have expressed disquiet about ceding sovereignty to Brussels. There's some irony underlying this: concern about sovereignty is greatest in England, but England, unlike Scotland, Wales, and Northern Ireland, with no political institutions of its own, is notoriously a nation without a state; a democratic deficit that seems to trouble almost no one. Some discontent has been economic: the free movement of goods, services, capital, and persons was all very well so long as the EU was made up of countries of broadly similar levels of prosperity, but the entry of several former Eastern Bloc countries has upset the equilibrium and made migration a significant part of many lives, some of whom perceive it as not a gift but a threat.

Which brings us to the third element of discontent: identity. Identity invariably rests on narrative. Britain has its own narrative, somewhat different from the mainstream European Union narrative. The European narrative is that the tension between France and Germany had caused a half-century of devastating war, and that the whole of Europe needed to gather round the two giants to forge a better future together, a future of economic prosperity based on free trade and on the emergence of a European entity to rival the United States, Russia, Japan, and in due course India and China. Britain's narrative is different. It's based on a memory of being in the vanguard of the Industrial Revolution, and at the head of a global empire, with a corresponding mixture of duty, superiority, and entitlement. Consider the song "Football's Coming Home." It keys into the sense that Britain (or England) invented all the games anyway, and has patiently let the upstarts win for much too long. But, in the twenty years after the Second World War, Britain became obsessed by the narrative of economic, political, and social decline. The question for Britain became whether membership of the EU reversed that decline, by charting a new, collaborative, confident identity—or epitomized that decline by allowing the grand old country to be swallowed up by a European leviathan.

One morning about a year ago, I was sitting in the green room at Broadcasting House, listening to the *Today* program, and waiting to offer my Thought for the Day when I was overwhelmed by the desire to walk into the studio, set aside my carefully constructed and minutely edited script, and simply say, "Let's face it everyone, Brexit may be a train crash but at least it's done what it was originally designed to do—unite the Tory party." There's no doubt that the Conservatives have been plagued by contrasting feelings on Europe for a generation, and the somewhat unexpected return of a Tory majority at the 2015 election meant that their quandary immediately became the nation's quandary. But the civil war in the party that's characterized the period since the triggering of Article 50 is an indication of the fact that the 52 percent leave vote in June 2016 was a temporary coalition of those whose opposition to EU membership was based on economic, political, and identity grounds. And as soon as Article 50 was triggered and the actual future relationship had to be defined, that coalition broke up into smithereens.

Christians have all kinds of political, social, and economic views, but for me the central question of our time is one of identity. Britain was taken into the EEC by Edward Heath with economic arguments that hid political commitments. David Cameron chose to fight the 2016 Brexit campaign on economic arguments, just as he had the Scottish independence vote two years previously. In both cases, I believe he fought the battle on the wrong territory. The real issue in both was identity. In my view, Remain deserved to lose the Brexit vote because it failed to describe a multicultural European vision that Britain would be in every way impoverished to leave. The trouble is, the Brexiteers have had two years to identify a restored British identity that was worth all this trouble to re-establish, and towards doing so they have made no progress whatsoever.

Not long ago I walked up to the Penshaw Monument near Houghton-le-Spring, and my companion pointed out the Nissan car factory whose workers overwhelmingly voted leave, even though they knew it would likely mean the eventual closure of the factory and the loss of thousands of jobs in County Durham. They weren't thinking about economics: they were thinking about identity. Those who were happiest the next day were glad because they had recaptured a glimpse of an identity they had feared was lost. Those who were saddest, and I include myself, were horrified because they didn't recognise themselves in that identity.

Christians may have a range of views about economics and politics, but faith is fundamentally about identity. Who are we? What are our lives for? What is Britain's future role in the world, as a small nation with a long history of punching way over its weight?

We live in a culture where such questions of ultimate purpose are seriously out of fashion. They are the territory on which the church should be very much at home, because the church has a very clear message of identity. That message is that our dignity derives from God's longing to be in relationship with us. Our freedom derives from Christ's Cross, in which he frees us from the curse of our past, the damage we've inflicted, and the hurt done to us. Our hope derives from Christ's Resurrection, in which he opens to us the promise and prospect of eternal life, releasing us from the prison of death. The purpose of life is therefore to exercise that freedom and build on that hope, creating communities that demonstrate the reconciliation they together make possible.

The Feast of All Saints is a moment we focus on those in the history of the church whose lives have shown us the character of the holy city that we've just heard about in Revelation 21. By describing our eternal home as a city, Revelation is telling us there will always be politics in our lives. We will always be in the business of making alliances with those we feel connected to and trying to persuade those whose differences from us lead to tension. There is no disembodied peace in which problems go away and honest dialogue is no longer required. That's not heaven–that's laziness. The saints show us the politics of heaven, which in this world continues to require sacrifice, courage, witness, and patience. Britain never completely got Europe right, and now it's about to embark on another chapter of how it relates to its international neighbors, near and far. Challenges and trials are sent to us to disclose who we really are and to reveal where our commitments truly lie. Only in the face of challenge do we discover gifts we never realized the Spirit was giving us. Right now the gift we as church and nation need is the grace to live with those who see the world very differently from the way we do.

That grace is a fruit of the Spirit too, along with the love, joy, and peace we'd rather be given.

This is the territory on which we need to be having the conversation, regardless of which negotiating position the government finally settles upon. What we're talking about is a diversity of visions of what it means to be human, what it means to join together with people who are different from ourselves, and how we can make a future together. June 23, 2016, exposed the fact that people have a variety of views on these things, far too wide in fact to be captured helpfully by a yes/no vote. But politics is about encompassing such diversity and making it fruitful, and it always has been. And so is church. We should have always known that.

The Brexit debate, both before the 2016 vote and even more since, has ignited gut-level feelings and soured otherwise amicable relationships like no other political issue in Britain in my lifetime. The outcome of the referendum took almost everyone by surprise, winner and losers, and what had not been anticipated was that a vote to leave the EU left a host of choices and unanswered questions that there was no obvious procedure available to resolve—particularly after the 2017 general election left the Conservative Party no majority in the House of Commons. Everyone is cross, almost no one has changed their mind about anything, and there seems (at the time of writing) no way out of the impasse.

At St Martin-in-the-Fields the mood in June 2016 was almost universally one of shock, sorrow, and bewilderment, and I and my clergy colleagues sought to reflect that mood in the days that followed the vote, particularly in light of our staff and congregation hailing from more than twenty-five different countries. But it quickly became clear that, while in the tiny minority, the Leavers were unapologetic, vocal, and assertive in the rightness of their cause, and that while almost overwhelming, the Remainers in the community could not take the universality of their convictions for granted, even in such a diverse and famously progressive environment. So for two years the subject went almost entirely unmentioned in sermons, and intercessions contained mysterious pleas that the Holy Spirit would "give wisdom to all exploring the future role of this country in relation to Europe and the rest of the world." Much the same culture was true of the Cambridge college, which voted overwhelmingly to remain, but among whose faculty were conspicuous, ardent, and articulate spokespeople and campaigners for the Leave cause. It was while reading a book written by one of these professors that I realized I was beginning to discover something that might need to be said that wasn't simply amplifying what everyone else was saying (and no one was listening to). I was also aware that, while its clergy had voted by a huge majority to remain, the laity of the Church of England had voted marginally to leave, and this was a reality with which the church as a whole was struggling to come to terms.

As I prepared the sermon, some things became clear. The first was that the theological point at stake was identity. In other words, this was, whether I made it explicit or not, fundamentally a sermon about baptism. The second was that in each the congregation would be apprehensive. There are so many ways to get things wrong when you are addressing a controversial subject, and few in either congregation seriously believed I would avoid all of the pitfalls. The most obvious pitfalls were these: to give the impression I was using the privilege of everyone's attention to tee off on my own personal prejudice, and inflict them on a captive congregation; to pretend I was neutral on a question on which I have yet to find a UK citizen who is neutral; to show no connection between my argument and the theological convictions and formation that had won me the honor of speaking from a pulpit; to suggest that those who disagreed with me were not only misguided but foolish and sinful; and, to lack the humility to recognize that I might be wrong. So I set about telling a story that would be genuinely interesting (and thus not incline the listener to feel I was merely repeating information endlessly discussed in the media), in which each person could locate themselves without too much difficulty, and that steered clear of the name-calling and reductionism of most of the debate. I then included an element of humor, not just to lighten the mood, but to introduce a note of reality about what the last forty years might have looked like from a non-UK perspective. Then, recognizing that the debate had been almost entirely on political and economic grounds, I made the single "great leap" of the sermon—to say that I didn't believe this was really about politics or economics, but about identity. This leap had to be established and argued; but once made, created the space to make two crucial points, both intended in an ecumenical, reconciling spirit. The first was that Christianity was about an identity that went deeper than national or any other ancillary identity. (The Cambridge sermon, being shorter, left out the part about All Saints, and this argument was weaker as a result.) The second was that politics is about navigating a host of different and sometimes conflicting identities, and church politics is not in most respects any different. If the first point was an invitation to all present to acknowledge a higher loyalty than their temporary divisions, the second point was designed to finish on a rather crestfallen note of humility that deep division shouldn't really be taking us by surprise. Success was going to be about persuasion, understanding, and grace, and never about pummeling the opposition into submission or regarding them as mad, bad, ignorant, or ridiculous.

It's always risky for the preacher to try to judge the reception of a sermon, so I relied on wise observers on each occasion to gauge the mood of the respective congregations. On both occasions there was such universal anxiety that I was going to fall into one or all of the five pitfalls noted earlier that the most tangible feeling afterwards was the relief and surprise that it seemed, to most, that I had not. I can't blame the Cambridge congregation for this, but I was still rather grieved that my regular congregation, whom I have served for six and a half years, were still anxious on this score. It simply shows how nervous a congregation is that a preacher will misuse the privilege of the pulpit—a nervousness only exacerbated when the subject matter is so notoriously divisive. The congregation can only have become so nervous from exposure to bad examples, in this setting or elsewhere. The second response in Cambridge was a more cheerful, "Well, something for everybody"—which initially seemed lame, but on reflection I took as gratifying, since it was a jovial reaction to a subject that has brought untold grief. The second response in London was a sense of pride, that people felt we were in a community where we could talk about difficult things in the light of shared faith and reach new insight born of close attention and careful restraint. The third response in Cambridge was delight that the much-maligned "church" could enter a public debate and have something fresh and helpful to add. The third response in London was negative: from the voice of the Leaver party who could only hear any reference to Brexit as a self-righteous preening of the righteousness of the Remain position, and couldn't seriously listen to the sermon for fear of receiving further wounding—wishing instead for further calls for reconciliation and unity.

I offer this as an experience from outside a US context from one who spent seven years preaching within the US milieu, and who, I trust, understands the differences as well as the congruences between the two. I dislike the term prophetic preaching (almost never used in the UK and, in my experience, unique to the US context), because it too often takes the virtue-signaling path dismantled by Jesus in his words about the Pharisee who went up to the temple to pray, and because it too quickly leaves scripture trailing behind in its specific policy proposals that are remarkably aligned with the platform of one particular political party. So many times I have heard the intercession "Lord may those in positions of authority take the guns out of the hands of those bent on slaughter, and help us to speak up in places where discrimination and prejudice abide." It's not that I have any admiration for US gun laws or any skin in the game of defending dis-crimination or prejudice, it's that such prayers could be translated (in *The Message* edition) as, "Lord, you exist to make the world more like us: hasten in your purpose."

I, therefore, in a quest to enrich pastoral preaching, offer in humility the following guidelines about taking on controversial subjects.

1. Get a reputation for your understanding and insight in scriptural exegesis, theological nuance, and pastoral depth before you take on edgy, divisive subjects outside the regular theological orbit. People really want to know about how to forgive and what to hope for when they die more than they want to know what the president should be doing about climate change. Remember a sermon is almost always about God. Revelation is about the new thing that God is showing us. Sermons are about revelation. So a sermon is about the new thing God is showing us—who God is, who we are, how the two are inextricably linked, and what to do about it.

2. Don't take on a big, weighty subject (like Brexit) more than one time in ten. And don't keep on and on about the same things. To make every sermon an attack on the president isn't prophetic, it's boring and predictable. And it's the fact that it's boring and predictable that demonstrates it's not the gospel, rather, it's politics. The gospel is never boring and predictable.

3. Don't be a "Saturday night preacher"—show your edgy sermon to trusted critics who will be able to suggest ways your deepest points may be more clearly heard and enable you to jettison material where your heart has overruled your head. Show it to those preparing music and prayers so a rounded perspective can be presented in the liturgy as a whole. Do your best to gauge the views of a dozen diverse congregation members in advance, to assess their fears and learn from their own investment in the issue, integrating their wisdom anonymously as appropriate.

4. Publicize your sermon theme in advance through website, email, and social media so that those for who the issue is sensitive (for example, on an issue such as abortion, should their life experience touch on it significantly) can keep their distance if they want or need to.

5. Avoid "glancing blows"—in other words, don't make stray references to big subjects in sermons that distract from whatever else you're saying and can't possibly do justice to a complex issue.

6. Don't pretend to be neutral when you're not. Part of what you're modeling is how to be gracious and perceptive even if you feel very strongly and are convinced right is on your side. If people are critical, courteously follow up with them and so discover ways in which you might be better able to understand and speak with your people.

7. Remember "the personal is the political"—in other words, it's more helpful to empower people to reflect on particular changes in their lives that together make a big difference, than to call on faraway people who aren't listening to change the world all at one go.

8. If you are so passionate about an issue that you can't speak charitably about those who take a different view and can't in any significant way present another perspective than your own, it may be best to handle a difficult subject through a town-hall or open-microphone-style meeting than through a sermon.

9. Never underestimate the diversity of even the most apparently monochrome congregation. Even when you are sure you are speaking "for us all" you almost certainly aren't, and if you are indeed speaking for us all it may not be necessary to speak at all. You can't call it prophetic if no one's disagreeing with you. Be very careful about using the word "we."

10. It shows no insight and no humility to call on everyone else to change but yourself. An argument caries a lot more weight if you say, "and I recognize to uphold this policy is going to require sacrifices from you and me." Actions speak louder than words. Don't advocate for more liberal migration laws without at the same time cultivating a policy for welcoming, integrating, or supporting migrants.

It's been said that the Episcopal Church is still grieving over discovering itself to have been on the wrong side of the civil rights movement of the 1960s and accordingly tending to overcompensation ever since. Even if it's only a half-truth, it goes some way towards explaining why prophetic preaching is such a significant issue for Episcopalians. It's nonsense to make a spiritual-material distinction and thus insist that church is for the soul and politics or public life is for the body. These are distinctions unknown to the Old Testament prophets and unrecognizable to Jesus. The problem with prophetic preaching is not that it's too often too prophetic, it's that it's too often terrible preaching—not about God, not new, not good news, not interesting, little or nothing to do with scripture, not about our own transformation. If we get the preaching right, the prophecy will most likely look after itself.

BIBLIOGRAPHY

Wells, Samuel. *Improvisation: The Drama of Christian Ethics*. 2nd edition. Grand Rapids: Baker, 2018.

Chapter 10

What Succeeds in Preaching
The Way of Blessing

Samuel G. Candler

Silence. You really are wonderful.

The most effective sermons we remember, or preach, often begin with these features: silence and honor. An effective preacher can begin their sermon by not saying anything, by simply standing before a congregation, by simply being there. In that silence, wonder begins to grow, and maybe even curiosity. Someone once said that the most attention any preacher ever has occurs in those quick silent moments before they even speak. If we want to gain people's attention, maybe the first act is to be quiet.

The second elegant—and pastoral—start to a sermon is to honor the listeners, even to praise the congregation, or the church, or the gathering. It may be selfish, or just natural, that most people enjoy being honored; we enjoy being praised, even when we realize that the praise is "just words." Of course, a sermon is much more than "just words." At any rate, honor and praise do gain the congregation's attention.

Remember, then, to gain the attention of your listener. It is a practical device. Getting attention is important—if you have something to say. If we preachers do not have anything to say, we should sit down. Please stop talking if you do not have anything to say.

Attention gained, what then should we do with it? Should we "preach politics"? My first response to that inquiry is to declare, "It's all politics." Despite a contemporary sense of the word—where politics is always partisan or manipulative or too involved in civic detail—I sense that politics is really about handling the ordering of the city or the community. That is exactly what parish leadership is, guiding and leading a community.

Successful preaching is one of the strongest ways a person leads a community of faith. Sermons are delivered within a pastoral perspective, and are always political. Furthermore, the world itself is the community of the preacher. The church. The local hospital. The circle of close friends. The world. All of it is our parish. Every sermon is both pastoral and prophetic in our community. Every successful sermon is "political"—it should measure what needs to be said with the community's identity and ability and lead the community in a journey towards salvation and service. And, every successful sermon occurs in relationship: it is communicated within a healthy and honest relationship.

A second response to the question is to tell a story. I serve a wonderful parish, the Cathedral Parish of St. Philip, in Atlanta, Georgia. It is quite large, and it is even more complicated than large. Soon after I first arrived as dean, I learned that the annual Peachtree Road Race in Atlanta, always held on the Fourth of July, would be on a Sunday morning that year. Other churches and ministers were also realizing that their Sunday morning services and routines would be severely disrupted by the closing of streets and some sixty thousand runners, wheelchair racers, and walkers pouring down Peachtree Street, the great backbone of the city of Atlanta. Newspaper articles and sermons lamented the interruption and even the loss of Sunday morning offering plate receipts. And, of course, whether one likes it or not, the Fourth of July is a political event in the United States of America.

When the director of the Atlanta Track Club made a personal visit to me, both to apologize and to explain the event, I resolved that we would not curse the race. As for my house, I said, we would bless and not curse. The director was relieved and even thrilled. So, I inquired as to whether she would mind if we moved our Sunday services to the street in order to welcome and bless all the runners. Of course, she said. So, I pressed further. Would it be acceptable for me to bless the runners by tossing holy water to, and upon, them as they ran by? And might we even arrange a hose and tall sprinkler, labeled "holy water" (which we blessed!) for the runners to run through? She agreed.

It was a grand and happy success. Thus was born a tradition that has continued at the Cathedral of St. Philip every year, whether the race occurs on a Sunday or not. We go to the street and bless over sixty thousand visitors to our church. "Blessings to you," I proclaim.

Blessings to Muslims: *Assalamu Alaikum*. Blessings to Jews: *Barukh atah Adonai, Eloheinu*. Blessings to Christians: Christ bless you. *Benedicite Deus*. To Hindus, to Buddhists, to atheists, to agnostics. God blesses each and every one of us. *Dios les bendiga*. I say all that and more, for almost three hours. When I bless the Peachtree Road Race, year after year, as sixty thousand people walk and run past our church within three hours, I am blessing all sorts of conditions, all of humanity in that wondrous event. To every tribe, people, and language: blessings to you! And the world, our parish, gets it.

When we speak to the world, our parish, we are often faced with the choice between cursing and blessing. Especially in divisive and antagonistic times, churches and parishes become known for cursing things or for blessing things. Indeed, some people attend church so that they can hear about what is wrong, about what needs condemning, about who is wrong, and about the way of cursing. Others go to church to hear blessing.

I realize, of course, that certain matters and issues need to be spoken against, but our habits are contagious. If we become known for cursing, we create cursing people. If we are known for blessing, we create blessing people. It may be that the most important thing we do in life is bless people.

Effective preaching, then, speaks from the perspectives of silence and blessing. Effective preaching speaks in the journey from silence to good words, and the journey from cursing to blessing. Effective preaching loves and serves the world; it does not condemn the world.

In the interest of organization, I have compiled my notes about successful preaching as principles. Some are imperatives, and not so much to others as to myself. I will number my points, my offerings, towards the goal of successful preaching, but there is no grand design, or plan, to the order. I offer these points as imperatives and as principles, but they are just holy ways. Sometimes, yes, one way takes precedence over another.

1. The Way of Blessing: Bless People. The first principle (to repeat) is to bless people. Blessing people, and especially blessing children, may be the most important vocation for any person, whether they are a preacher or not, whether ordained or not, whether a parent or not. The world is our parish, and the world needs blessing. The word "blessing" can have several definitions. One definition is a "good word," in the same way that the word "benediction," means "good word." Give good words to people. Give good words to a world that suffers from a lack of them.

One of the horrifying consequences of poor politics is the misuse of words by politicians and leaders, and then, the poor use of words or the inaccurate use of words. The political world does not need any more poorly-used or misused words. The world needs more good words: benedictions, blessings.

2. The Way of Self-Knowledge: Know Yourself. The old Delphic maxim holds: the most important thing any preacher can offer is ourselves, that is, our authentic selves. When we preach well, we are delivering our truest selves. Listeners can recognize when a preacher is sharing their true self. Sometimes the sermon can be a tangled, illogical mess, yet, when listeners recognize authenticity, God speaks even in our ineptitude.

Phillips Brooks, a nineteenth-century rector of Trinity Church, Boston, once gave a definition of preaching as "truth through personality." The truth of God's word delivers itself through the person of the preacher. That particular person is me; the better I know that particular person (myself), the better I will deliver truth.

When I counsel couples who are about to exchange marriage vows, I give the same advice. The most important element you bring to this marriage is an understanding of who you truly are, your true self. If you are not giving away, or committing, your true self, then your partner is not understanding, or receiving, your true self. Somewhat like a marriage, an effective sermon communicates and gives your true self, not your false self.

Finally, of course, our true self is the one that is found in Christ, the living and incarnate truth of God. But we don't lose our individual personalities in that identity with Christ. We preach from the Christ in us, the hope of glory.

3. The Way of Love: Love Your People. Love is what people are truly looking for, whether they realize it or not. Parish ministry itself needs this principle. Sometimes, it does not even matter whether the minister carries any specific talents or gifts. If there is any grand secret to parish ministry as a whole, it is to "show up and love your people." That is also a principle of good preaching. It is a principle of good political preaching. People can discern whether the preacher loves their people.

Preaching creates character. However, I do not refer simply to what the words of the sermon are saying. I mean that the way a preacher preaches models a particular character for the congregation. The attitude, demeanor, tone, and character of the preacher are all communicative. The way we preach can actually create the character and personality of our community. Sermons create character.

As he was studying the Book of Psalms, Augustine of Hippo realized an intriguing feature of how humanity understands God, a feature that leads to how congregations might interpret preachers. Consider Psalm 18:25–56:

> With the loyal you show yourself loyal:
> with the blameless you show yourself blameless:
> with the pure you show yourself pure;
> and with the crooked you show yourself perverse.

In the same manner as this psalm, I believe Augustine suggests that there is something about our demeanor, our character, that shapes how we will interpret God. In his *Exposition on the Book of Psalms*, Augustine says:

> "With the holy Thou shalt be holy" (verse 25). There is a hidden depth also, wherein Thou art known to be holy with the holy, for that Thou makest holy. "And with the harmless Thou shalt be harmless." For Thou harmest no man, but each one is bound by the bands of his own sins. "And with the chosen Thou shalt be chosen" (ver. 26). And by him whom Thou choosest, Thou art chosen. "And with the froward Thou shalt be froward." And with the froward Thou seemest froward: for they say, "The way of the Lord is not right:" and their way is not right.[1]

"Thou art known to be holy with the holy," Augustine said. Extending that principle, I suggest that the manner of our preaching with a con-

---

1. St. Augustine of Hippo, *Expositions on the Book of Psalms,* ed. P. Schaff, trans. A.C. Coxe (New York: Christian Literature Company, 1888), vol. 8:52.

gregation (the conversation the preacher has with the congregation) creates different types of community. Consequentially, people will behave towards the preacher in the same ways the preacher behaves towards them. If we tell people how bad they are, they will tell us how bad we are. If we tell people our stories, then people will tell us their stories. If we tell people how to vote, then people will tell us how to vote. If preachers are humble, they model humility for the listener. On the other hand, if we tell people the mistakes we have made, they will tell us the mistakes they have made. If we love people, they will love people. Anger begets anger; love begets love.

If preachers want listeners to change their minds, preachers would do well to show people how we (we preachers) have changed our own minds. Congregations who have appreciated hearing how preachers have changed their minds are therefore given a model and example of how to change.

4. The Way of Text-Knowledge: Know the Text. In Christian preaching, when the lectionary gives us the text, it is worth knowing the Bible. Know your Bible, and its holy texts.

I am fortunate to have been preaching in the same congregation for twenty years, and I cannot remember an instance when I have not used one of the lectionary texts as the theme, or starting point, for my sermon. Our scriptural texts are authoritative for me. One of the advantages of a long tenure is that I have had time to cover many biblical texts; I do not have to say everything in one sermon.

Indeed, preaching from all of scripture is critical to our faithful preaching. When we dare to interpret the Bible, we are touching the genetic depth of our Christian identity; we are touching our Christian DNA. Be careful with it. But a sermon setting contains other texts, as well. The preacher may have been engaging the lectionary text all week, but the average congregation will have spent as much time engaging other texts: the news of politics, of the community, of the culture. Sometimes the parish wants us to preach on the same texts that they have been hearing all week, but sometimes they don't. Even though congregations usually appreciate our awareness of these other texts, the Christian preacher ultimately depends upon a text that is different from, and greater than, the texts of the world.

One of the most fascinating features of the Bible, as a large collection of writings, is that the Bible interprets itself, over time. The Bible is not an absolutist document, but a conversation. Different writers reinterpret what others have said previously in scripture. The Hebrew scriptures, for instance, search for the identity of Yahweh, as compared to El and Elohim. Some of the prophets don't like the temple, but later prophets urge that tithes be collected for the temple. It's an ancient and delightful conversation that is always political.

Jesus was a master reinterpreter: "You have heard it said . . . but I say unto you . . ." He was continuing the long and sacred conversation. When someone asked Jesus what the greatest law might be, he did not avoid the question by saying, "Oh my, they are all equally valid." No, he boldly claimed that the commandment about loving God was the greatest (Deut. 6:5), and the second one was like it: "Love your neighbor as yourself" (Lev. 19:18).

The preacher does well to emphasize some parts of scripture over others, because that is what our biblical ancestors have done. Yes, we have a sacred treasure in the scripture, but it is not simply a book of equally valid claims; the Bible is a sacred conversation. Be a part of the informed conversation.

There is another text within which I work, which is the Anglican tradition itself. In fact, I prefer to use the term, "Anglican tradition," rather than what I sense is the more limited "Episcopal tradition." My parish knows that I resist the phrase "middle way" as a definition of our tradition. The Episcopal Church, the Anglican tradition, is not the *via media*. Rather, our tradition is what I have come to describe as the "*via comprehensiva*," or the "Comprehensive Way." Over and over again in our tradition's history, we have navigated sensitive theological and social controversies by expanding our embrace, by truly trying to cover both sides of the road. I resist the description of our tradition as a "middle way" because that surrender seems all too often to ineptly and awkwardly place us in the muddy middle of the road. I have heard it said that "people standing in the middle of the road get hit by traffic coming from both directions."

My sense of the Anglican tradition, at our best, is that we try to cover both sides of the road, even when they seem oppositional. Beginning with the sixth- and seventh-century conflict in the British Isles between local Celtic authority and universal Roman authority, the Anglican tradition has lived with, and embraced, differing sides of conflicts over authority that appeared antagonistic to most.

If any one person (besides Jesus Christ) is responsible for the identity of the Anglican tradition, it was certainly not Henry VIII, who was always quite Roman in his theology; it was Queen Elizabeth I, who embraced both Roman and Protestant forms of the Christian faith. Hers was the *via comprehensiva*, the comprehensive way.

Later, in the United States in the nineteenth century, the Episcopalian William Porcher DuBose said:

> The one great lesson that must forerun and make ready the Christian unity of the future is this: that contraries do not necessarily contradict, nor need opposites always oppose. What we want is not to surrender or abolish our differences, but to unite and compose them. We need the truth of every variant opinion and the light from every opposite point of view. The least fragment is right in so far as it stands for a part of the *truth*.[2]

DuBose is describing the *via comprehensiva*. Those lines also describe how faithful Anglicans and Episcopalians have preached, generation after generation. It is the entire sacred conversation of scripture that is authoritative for us. There is not one text that is authoritative—though, if I had to offer only one guiding verse for me, it would be Paul's 1 Corinthians 15:22, "For as in Adam all die, even so in Christ all shall be made alive" (NKJV).

5. The Way of Work: Do Your Homework at Home, Not in the Public Sermon. I refer, of course, to the details of our scriptural exegesis and research. Some of the most boring sermons we have heard begin with some kind of wandering words like, "When I was wondering about what I should preach about this Sunday . . . ," and then the preacher wanders around their subconscious a while, or the preacher begins by rehearsing all of their pointless research.

Yes, the listener needs for the preacher to have done that work, but the listener does not need to hear about it. A delivered sermon is like

2. William Porcher DuBose, *The Gospel in the Gospels* (New York: Longmans, Green, & Co., 1906), ix.

wearing clothes. We want you to have put on your undergarments first. We want them to be there, but we don't want to see them. We want to see the finished result of your dressing. People don't really want to see our underwear.

6. The Way of Movement: The Purpose of a Sermon Is to Move People. The purpose of the sermon is not simply to say something. A sermon is a form of leadership, and good leadership is about getting people to move somewhere. Any person, these days, can tweet a few characters; real leadership moves people. Especially when participating in a politically charged environment, the preacher's real work is to move people, not to register their vote. Effective leadership occurs in healthy relationship; a successful preacher has a relationship, a moving relationship, with the congregation.

In a sermon the "moving" can occur in several ways. There is emotional movement, for sure. Effective sermons are delivered with healthy emotional range. Principles of rhetoric and public speaking can help the preacher. But there is also intellectual movement. An effective sermon can move our intellects, our passions, our spirits.

Thus, an effective sermon begins at a particular point. It acknowledges reality in one place, but then it moves us somewhere else. The preacher takes us somewhere. Even if the preacher ends up returning to where we started, they have taken us on a journey. Most people want to be moved. It's why we read books or go to the movies; it is also why we listen to sermons.

In an effective sermon, there is probably only one major movement, one major point of the sermon. In a fun sermon, every twist and turn has its own moment too. Maybe the wonderful and awesome sermon is like a big weather front, or a thunderstorm. There is one huge storm, or even one major twister funnel, but there are also lots of little twisters moving around as well. Those side events can be fine. Sometimes they are what our listeners remember. They get distracted and enjoy it. The Holy Spirit can direct all sorts of winds.

7. The Way of Vision: See Something. This point seems obvious, but it is worth noting. The effective and pastoral preacher should have something to say, and they should be confident and clear about it, but imaginatively presenting the point is another step entirely for the effective preacher. Be imaginative. Imagine. Consider the theological principle, or the prophetic point, or the pastoral comfort that you want to emphasize that day and present it with creativity. Which brings us to the next point.

8. The Way of Formation: Shape the Sermon. It takes a lot of experience for a veteran preacher to be able to just turn on the tap, let water run out, and have every stream be valuable and filling and wonderful and satisfactory. The experience comes from hours and years of shaping ideas and words and paragraphs and pages. For most of us, the direct-to-page, stream-of-consciousness sermon does not work. Perhaps it works as a kind of journaling exercise, but it often fails to engage listeners.

Another way of saying this is that most of us cannot simply sit at the piano, start playing, and come up with a sonata. A sonata takes practice and time. It takes shaping. It takes composing, editing, and throwing stuff away.

Throw some stuff away. That is why it is good to have a time limit, or a page limit, to sermons. Compose a lot more than is necessary, and then throw a lot of it away.

9. The Way of Practice: Practice. Practice your scales. I play a lot of jazz piano, and I actually do sometimes sit at the piano and just turn on the tap. Jazz music, of course, consists of a lot of improvising. But that jazz does not simply occur by magic. It takes practice.

As a pianist, I had to learn the musical scales. I still practice the scales. For the most part, the scales are not interesting, but they are the foundation. Out of the tedious scales can come, with God's grace, some fun music. It is the same way with sermons and words. As the preacher practices the words, and the Word, the sermon takes shape.

In some parts of the African American church, it is common practice for the host pastor to call out a guest preacher and ask if they have a word for the congregation. When entering any preaching and worshipping community, it is good to have a sermon ready. That is practice.

I remember a rector of a large church with several assistants and curates who required all his assistants to have a sermon prepared each

Sunday. Only one of them would actually preach that day, but no one knew who it would be. Only minutes before the service would he choose a preacher for that day. They all had a word for the congregation. They were all practicing.

Much of what the preacher, pastor, or even prophet does is lead the people of God in practice, maybe like an athletic coach, every day. Practice moving people closer to the grace of God. In my own parish, we talk incessantly, not about a mission statement, but about principles and values. Our values are grace, excellence, and hospitality. We serve the gospel of Jesus Christ with grace, excellence, and hospitality. Thus, our preaching is about practicing those values everywhere.

10. The Way of Blessing: Bless People. Again. In her beautiful novel *Gilead,* Marilynne Robinson tells the story of a dying seventy-six-year-old minister who is writing words for his seven-year-old son. They are the words (the "good words") he wants his son to remember. Early in the book, he says, "There is a reality in blessing, which I take baptism to be, primarily. It doesn't enhance sacredness, but it acknowledges it, and there is a power in that."[3] Later, when he is asking himself whether he ought to bless someone, someone about whom he has doubts, he reflects, "Transformations [quite] abrupt do occur in this life, and they occur unsought and unawaited . . . . The Lord is constant. Wherever you turn your eyes the world can shine like transfiguration. You don't have to bring a thing to it except a little willingness to see. Only, who could have the courage to see it?"[4]

Effective preachers have the courage to see. We have the courage to bless. And, when we bless someone—when we speak good words to them, when we touch them with God's grace—they become transfigured into the grace of a child of God. Sometimes, our blessings might feel like tired routines, like playing musical scales over and over again at the piano. True blessing really does take work.

On November 13, 2016, the Sunday after Donald Trump was elected president of the United States, I preached. The country, and my congregation, had been living in and with a huge and complicated

3. Marilynne Robinson, *Gilead* (New York: Picador, 2004), 23.
4. Robinson, *Gilead,* 203, 245.

text. How does a Christian successfully preach after that day? One of the advantages I had was my history of relationships in that place. People knew me, and they probably knew my politics; but, they also knew that I do not normally speak directly to our country's politics. Again, my politics, and my preaching, are relational. I can say what I say only in the context of an ongoing and loving relationship within my community of faith.

But there were other texts that day. Our lectionary presented the words of the prophet Isaiah: "For I am about to create new heavens and a new earth; the former things shall not be remembered or come to mind" (Isa. 65:17). Finally, for me it was the Sunday after my hero, Leonard Cohen, had died; he had died on the night before the election. I realized, of course, that much of my congregation did not follow Leonard Cohen, or even know who he was, but people who knew me knew of my affection for Cohen; and, for that matter, they probably knew how I had voted in the national elections. His poetry became a striking symbol for that week.

Whether the sermon was successful or not, I tried to preach on all the texts. Because some of my preaching principles might be featured in this sermon, I close this essay with some paragraphs from it.

There Is a Crack in Everything

*A sermon preached at the Cathedral of St. Philip,
Atlanta, on November 13, 2016*

People have said that they take the comments and character of our president-elect "seriously but not literally." Well, that's a phrase I usually like. I say that about the Bible a lot: "Take it seriously, but not always literally." But words matter. One cannot throw words into the public arena and then pretend they don't exist, or pretend they were a joke. It takes a long time to repair mean words.

I do not think that such behavior is the new heaven and the new earth that God is talking about in the Bible. Biblical virtues take a long time to develop. Character takes a long time to build.

Yes, what a week. I understand that new life always seems to involve something old passing away. But, I would rather be preaching about the death of my hero, Leonard Cohen, the poet and musician who died this past week. He was able somehow to communicate the deep light of life that appears even in deep darkness. God resides in the darkness, in the cracks, in the beautiful losers. He sang, "Everybody knows the war is over; everybody knows the good guys lost. Everybody knows the fight is fixed; the poor stay poor, the rich get rich. That's how it goes. Everybody knows."[5]

Cohen's words were the most humble, the most lowly of words. People considered him despondent, but he knew how to dance–he knew how to dance to the end of love. So long, Marianne. So long, Leonard, a sportsman and a shepherd. "Hineni, hineni," he sang in Hebrew. "Here I am; I am ready, Lord," he sang just days before his death. . . .[6]

This week demands that we be on record–that we witness for what we believe–as individuals and as the Christian church. My witness is that most of the changes in this country have been for the better, not for the worse. The United States of America is a strong country because we are against racism, and we are against using racism to advance popularity. We are against the abuse and ill treatment of women. We are against the mistrust of foreigners. And, this is the claim of the Christian church, too. We are against accusations without evidence; we call that false witness.

As a Christian, I am for much more. I am for the equal treatment of God's great diversity of people in this country, for the dignity of blacks and whites, Christians, Jews, and Muslims. We call it dignity and respect for God's creation. Christians are for other great new things in our country, too. I am for same-sex marriage. I am for women's reproductive rights. I am for the welcome of immigrants. . . .

---

5. Leonard Cohen and Sharon Robinson, "Everybody Knows," from the album *I'm Your Man* (February 1988).

6. Leonard Cohen, "You Want it Darker," from the album *You Want It Darker* (October 2016).

I am glad, and proud, to be in a Christian church and in this particular church, the Cathedral Parish of St. Philip. We belong to a communion that is larger, and older, and more expansive even than our own country. We gather together because we know that God is faithful when we make the right choices, and God is faithful when we make the wrong choices.

We serve for the long term, because we know that virtue takes a lifetime to create. Good character is built over a lifetime. We are trying to be a part of God's new creation, long term. We do not shame people in this community. We do not intentionally embarrass people. We respect all of God's creation here. We dignify all people. Like Cohen, "we tell the truth, we didn't come to fool ya."[7] We know we have cracks. We know we are weak. But, we know God is strong.

We allow many voices here, but we do not let people rest simply upon their own opinions. We speak another opinion too, the one that is for the common good, the long-term good, the virtuous good, the new creation good of God. We are the Body of Christ, the one who said, "I am among you as one who serves" (Luke 22:27). We want to be that light—the light of the world—that is getting in through the cracks. That is why we sing our song. That is why, even at the grave, we make our song, "Hallelujah, Hallelujah, Hallelujah." Amen.

My sermons are not usually so direct about countries or elections. Some people were offended. Some walked out. Some people loved it. However, for me it was another occasion to remember that blessing is the most important thing we do, that blessing takes a lot of practice, and that blessing takes a long time.

A little over two years after that national election, the Republican candidate for governor of Georgia, Brian Kemp, was elected. Partisan controversy seeped through the campaigning and the election. However, it was generally acknowledged by both sides that Kemp benefitted a great deal from the endorsement of Donald Trump. The office

---

7. Leonard Cohen, "Hallelujah," from the album, *Various Positions* (June 1984).

of Brian Kemp, a faithful Episcopalian, contacted me to inquire if I would host his inauguration day prayer service at the Cathedral of St. Philip, which is in the same neighborhood as the governor's mansion. Of course, I said. Of course, we would. And we did. It is our practice to bless people.

> Practice blessing people. In our tradition, blessing bears fruit.
> The Lord bless you and keep you.
> The Lord make his face to shine upon you and be gracious to you.
> The Lord lift up his countenance upon you, and give you peace.

AMEN.

BIBLIOGRAPHY

DuBose, William Porcher. *The Gospel in the Gospels*. New York: Longmans, Green, & Co., 1906.

Robinson, Marilynne. *Gilead*. New York: Picador, 2004.

St. Augustine of Hippo. *Expositions on the Book of Psalms*. Edited by P. Schaff. Translated by A.C. Coxe. Vol. 8. New York: Christian Literature Company, 1888.

Chapter 11

Last Word
Reimagining Prophetic Preaching
Mark Jefferson

It is essential to understand the imagination as critical to the enterprise of preaching and the identity of the preacher. Noted preacher and scholar of preaching Barbara Brown Taylor, argues, "The church's central task is an imaginative one. By that, I do not mean a fanciful or fictional task, but one in which the human capacity to imagine—to form mental pictures of the self, the neighbor, the world, the future, to envision new realities—is both engaged and transformed."[1] The institution of the church and the people who are the church assemble in an experience of the imagination. The purposes of the experience are engagement and transformation of the imagination.

Taylor states that everyone has imagination, but through the process of socialization and notions of reality, many people operate within a dilapidated imagination. Evidence of imaginative dilapidation is how a child's "imagination thrives on the sensual details that their elders have learned to take for granted."[2] Therefore, the imagination or the process for re-imagination is, "a process of conversion—or reconversion—a recovery of what we once knew and forgot."[3] This is true for how humans understand themselves. Taylor states, "Wittingly or unwittingly, we human beings are driven by our images of ourselves, of other people, of God and the world—images that come to us both from within and without."[4]

---

1. Barbara Brown Taylor, *The Preaching Life* (Boston: Cowley Publications, 1993), 41.
2. Ibid., 42.
3. Ibid., 43.
4. Ibid.

The culture and its symbols influence the imagination, especially religious images and iconography, as these totems invite the imagination to reconsider the certain and question the boundaries of so-called reality. The power to conceive and manifest through words is a form of conjure with a caveat: "Are we really prepared to confess that God is the property of our imaginations? No. But we may be prepared to confess that our imaginations are the property of God."[5] The ability of humans to create a picture in their mind of something that is imperceptible to the tangible world and experience it in such a visceral way to the point where there is a limited distinction between conceptual and actual reality must be renewed and converted. The image of the Talented Tenth,[6] which began as an outlier image, became predominant in black preaching. The human imagination is not static, but in fact "turns out to be a place where vision is formed and reformed, where human beings encounter an inner reality with the power to transform the other realities of life."[7]

The imagination is a place of hope and challenge. Taylor testifies to the imagination being an unending source of enchantment. The process of imagining or reimagining allows her "to find the hidden figures, to confront the ordinary in full confidence that would yield the extraordinary if only I looked hard enough if only I kept at it and did not give up."[8] This tenacity of imagination requires a giving up of "the notion that I know what I am looking at when I look at the world."[9] The process of reimagining is a process of recovery that requires the humility and curiosity to set aside the "reality" of the present world to conceive other "realities" and images. The preacher becomes a metaphor and engages in metaphorical and symbolic play for the effective and holistic development of the congregation. The future of churches and the

---

5. Ibid., 46.

6. The Talented Tenth refers to the concept imagined by W.E.B. Du Bois (and first appearing in Du Bois's *The Negro Problem*), emphasizing the necessity of leadership development amongst the top 10 percent of black Americans. "Talented Tenth," Encyclopedia Britannica, https://www.britannica.com/topic/Talented-Tenth (accessed April 9, 2019).

7. Taylor, *The Preaching Life*, 49.

8. Ibid., 52.

9. Ibid.

preachers who serve them is connected to the ability of scholars to help conceive new preaching realities by offering lively and pertinent metaphors for the preacher to reimagine the practices of preaching.

The use of metaphor—the juxtaposing of contrasting images for comparison and contrast—is a powerful tool for reimagining preaching. It is little wonder that thinking of the preacher as a witness, a herald, a shepherd, a midwife, a fool, an emcee, or another image employs metaphorical language. Exploring and developing the implications of these metaphors allow for the construction of new homiletic theories. There are significant works that discuss the concept of metaphor—including Janet Soskice's *Metaphors and Religious Language*—and call for a more expansive rhetorical and literary consideration for metaphor, but, for this discussion, George Lakoff and Mark Johnson's seminal work *Metaphors We Live By* provides a helpful way to understand metaphor leading to a reimagining of homiletics.[10]

Lakoff and Johnson's significant contribution is to recover metaphor from a narrow construal within literature. The authors forward the notion of metaphoric engagement by foregrounding the cognitive and behavioral aspects of metaphor, arguing that metaphor is more than just a figure of speech that places two incredible images in a linguistic relationship by speaking about one thing in a manner that is used to describe or discuss the other. The concept of metaphor has often remained unexplored within the realm of language alone, disconnected from its implications about how metaphors operate upon consciousness and how they manifest in the world. Lakoff and Johnson assert, "Our ordinary conceptual system, in terms of which we both think and act, is metaphorical. The concepts that govern our thought are not just matters of the intellect. They also govern our everyday functioning, down to the most mundane details."[11] Metaphors are not merely functions of language. They order our lives in ways that are conscious and unconscious. Lakoff and Johnson posit that metaphors "structure what we perceive, how we get around in the world, and how we relate to other people. Our conceptual system thus plays a central

---

10. George Lakoff and Mark Johnson, *Metaphors We Live By* (Chicago: University of Chicago, 1980).

11. Lakoff and Johnson, *Metaphors We Live By*, 3.

role in defining our everyday realities . . . what we do every day is very much a matter of metaphor."[12] Language becomes *evidence* of how metaphors *work* instead of merely what metaphors may *say.*

Metaphors work as an internal narrative or system of narratives because "human thought processes" are largely metaphorical.[13] The images carry within themselves an internal logic that the consciousness finds relevant for comparison for self-understanding. The expression of a metaphor becomes linguistic evidence of a larger consciousness of the person. "Metaphors as linguistic expressions are possible precisely because there are metaphors in a person's conceptual system."[14] Humans are what they imagine themselves to be, and pictures or images are central to that act. Homiletician Warren Wiersbe also discerns the power of metaphor:

> One of the bridges between the world around us and the world within us is a system of symbols that we call language, and language is metaphorical. It communicates in *pictures.* God's creation is a theater, and the human mind is a picture gallery, and we link the two by using words.[15]

The metaphorical language people use is a function of mediating the internal "picture gallery" with the "theater" of the outside context. Wiersbe comments, "Since preachers want their people to learn, to think, and to have new and maturing experiences, they had better get acquainted with this thing called metaphor."[16]

For Lakoff and Johnson, humans conceive of themselves in metaphor, and their conceptual framework is image-based–metaphorical. The conceptual metaphor is not just an idea, but "plays a central role in defining everyday realities."[17] Thus, new metaphors must be created to change the dominant approach defining the realities of everyday

---

12. Ibid.

13. Ibid., 6.

14. Ibid.

15. Warren W. Wiersbe, *Preaching and Teaching with Imagination: The Quest for Biblical Ministry* (Grand Rapids: Baker Books, 1994), 41.

16. Wiersbe, *Preaching and Teaching with Imagination,* 42.

17. Ibid.

life. A conceptual metaphor not only provides a visual image but also informs behavior. Metaphors are systemic: "Because the metaphorical concept is systemic, the language we use to talk that aspect of the concept is systemic."[18] A conceptual metaphor has within itself an internal logic of actions and ideas that define it. The use of metaphor provides an expectation of action. Those actions are logical and systematic because of how semantic entailment operates. The constant usage of the same metaphors can lead to habituated action and the calcification of the imagination. The field of homiletics continues to reimagine itself through the process of conjuring images and metaphors for the preacher. Seeking to avoid the staleness that happens to even the sturdiest of images, scholars of preaching continue to offer new conceptual metaphors for the preacher for the reimagining of preaching. In this endeavor, I am no different.

There are benefits and inherent limitations of the use of metaphorical language to understand the role of the preacher. Namely, as much as metaphors illuminate and re-convert the imagination, they are also partial, fleeting, and brittle. No one metaphor encapsulates everything; therefore, an array of metaphors is active in a person's imagination. The strength of a metaphor is in its fragility. A tenuous dependence is built into the structure of a metaphor as it depends upon its relevance to the experience of the person. A fresh metaphor can quicken the mind and enliven the body through an alternate angle of inner vision. A conceptual metaphor, at its best, opens the windows of the imagination and circulates a fresh breeze of embodied possibility. A limitation of metaphors is that they are only as powerful as they are relevant. No single metaphor can encompass the fullness of the human experience. Thus, art quests after fresh ways to encounter the beauty of everyday life. As times change, symbols acquire new and layered meanings, and metaphors require revisiting according to usefulness. As much as metaphors disclose new concepts of self-expression and originality, new metaphors are always present, offering fresh perspectives to trusted imaginings and conceptions.

The contributors to this book provide different images and visions for prophetic preaching, or put differently, preaching politics. The

---

18. Lakoff and Johnson, *Metaphors We Live By*, 7.

complexity of issues surrounding the words "politics" and "preaching" present the current consciousness in preaching with a new opportunity for action. Further, they provoke the development of new images and production of a new vocabulary concerning God's intention for humanity. Prophets are not only those who are spoken of in the Hebrew Bible or the New Testament; they are active among us and in us. God is calling preachers to be bold in their declaration and fervent in their supplication, which deepens their proclamation. May we follow Jesus into the way of preaching so that politics would never be the same again.

BIBLIOGRAPHY

Lakoff, George and Mark Johnson. *Metaphors We Live By*. Chicago: University of Chicago, 1980.

"Talented Tenth." Encyclopaedia Britannica. https://www.britannica. com/topic/Talented-Tenth. Accessed April 9, 2019.

Taylor, Barbara Brown. *The Preaching Life*. Boston: Cowley Publications, 1993.

Wiersbe, Warren W. *Preaching and Teaching with Imagination: The Quest for Biblical Ministry*. Grand Rapids: Baker Books, 1994.

Acknowledgments

The editors are grateful to Nancy Bryan and Church Publishing for seeing the potential in the project. We are honored by your trust. We are also grateful to the contributors to this project. Thank you for committing your time and immense talents.

From Ian Markham

Every book project is special. It was at lunch one day in the refectory at Virginia Theological Seminary that Crystal wanted to discuss prophetic preaching with me. As we talked, we both agreed that this was a book. She was game. Crystal is organized, fun, deeply intelligent, and committed to a faith grounded in the Episcopal tradition and with a passion for Jesus. She did all the hard work. For the idea, talent, and hard work, I'm grateful. This collection of essays is also the result of countless, often agonized, conversations that have been shared in restaurants and bars around the country and around the world. I am grateful to my senior team who make the possibility of writing an option: Melody Knowles, Jacqui Ballou, Katie Glover, Linda Dienno, and Jim Mathes. Three administrative assistants helped with this project. It started under Katherine Malloy, continued under Karen Anderson, and concluded under Cassandra Gravina. Each made a major difference in the project. A key conversation partner is my son, Luke Markham, who brings joy to Lesley and me every day. And once again, Lesley, my wife, allowed the home to be the venue for a fabulous conversation around some of the hardest issues facing the church today. Thank you, Lesley.

From Crystal Hardin

This book was a labor of love. I am indebted to Ian for seeing its potential and for recognizing in me the ability to bring such a project to fruition. For your encouragement, wisdom, good humor, and faith, Ian, you have my sincere gratitude. I am grateful to those in the student body at Virginia Theological Seminary who put up with (and chimed in on) my incessant talking about prophetic and political preaching—especially those students who went as pilgrims to Jerusalem with me in January, 2019. Thank you for your patience, support, and good humor while I wrote my chapter (ten words at a time) as we traveled the Holy Land. To the friends who attended the in-person gathering of contributors—Alyse Viggiano, Elizabeth Henry-McKeever, Melesa Skoglund, Jonathan Pucik—your engagement was invaluable to the conversation and helped shape this book into what it is now. Thank you. Elizabeth Henry-McKeever, for your support and skillful editing, I cannot thank you enough. I am also indebted to my lay committee at Christ Church, Georgetown, for being insightful and supportive conversation partners on the topic of prophetic and political preaching, and to the Reverend Elizabeth Keeler for her steady and wise mentorship. I am better, and this book is better, for it. Finally, to my husband, Bradford, and my daughters, Lillian and Eliot, I extend all my love and gratitude. You make it all possible and all worthwhile. Bradford, for your tireless support, valuable insight, and endless good humor, I could never thank you enough.

Contributors

Samuel G. Candler is dean of the Cathedral of St. Philip in Atlanta, Georgia. He previously served as dean of Trinity Cathedral in Columbia, South Carolina, where he was a member of the Governor's Commission on Race Relations. He currently serves on the Task Force on Liturgical and Prayer Book Revision for the Episcopal Church. He has lectured and preached in England, Costa Rica, Canada, and across the United States. He is committed to interfaith relationships of good faith, and he helped establish the Faith Alliance (the interfaith network in Atlanta) and World Pilgrims (a group committed to taking Jews, Christians, and Muslins on interfaith pilgrimages). He serves on a variety of boards and organizations, including the Westminster Schools in Atlanta, and has served on the board of trustees of the Berkeley Divinity School at Yale University and of the Compass Rose Society of the Anglican Communion. He writes a commentary called "Good Faith and the Common Good" and is a contributor to the Episcopal Cafe and to *Day1*, a national weekly ecumenical radio show. He graduated magna cum laude from Yale University Divinity School (and Berkeley Divinity School at Yale, its Episcopal component) in 1982.

Sarah T. Condon is diocesan missioner to Rice University in Houston, Texas. She formerly served as assistant for pastoral care at St. Martin's Episcopal Church, Houston. She is the author of *Churchy: The Real Life Adventures of a Wife, Mom and Priest* (Mockingbird Ministries, 2016), an associate editor of the Mockingbird blog, and co-host of *The Mockingcast.* She is a frequent contributor to the popular Mockingbird ministry, which seeks to connect the Christian faith with realties of everyday life in fresh and down-to-earth ways. She received a master of divinity degree from Yale Divinity School in 2013.

Alex Dyer is canon to the ordinary for the Diocese of Colorado. He was formerly the priest-in-charge at St. Thomas' Parish, located in the Dupont Circle neighborhood of Washington, DC. He started his ministry as a missionary in Cairo, Egypt, working with Sudanese refugees. Since then, he has served numerous parishes in New York City and Connecticut. He has a heart for urban ministry which began with his time at St. Luke in the Fields, New York City, where he oversaw outreach programs for LGBT youth and a program for people with HIV/AIDS. During his career, he has served as executive director of the largest food pantry in New Haven, Connecticut, as a deputy to General Convention, as a member of the search committee for the bishop of Connecticut, as a member of the Commission on Ministry for the Episcopal Church in Connecticut, and as the president of the Standing Committee in the Episcopal Church in Connecticut.

Crystal J. Hardin serves as assistant to the rector at Christ Church, Georgetown, in Washington, DC, and is canonically resident in the Diocese of Virginia. She graduated magna cum laude from the University of Alabama School of Law in 2008, where she was awarded Order of the Coif honors, named a Hugo L. Black Scholar, and served as an editor of the *Alabama Law Review*. She received her master of divinity degree summa cum laude from Virginia Theological Seminary in 2019.

Ruthanna Hooke is the associate dean of chapel and the associate professor of homiletics at Virginia Theological Seminary. In addition, she leads workshops and retreats focusing on performance and vocal training for clergy and parishes. She serves as adjunct clergy at St. Thomas' Parish, Washington, DC, and on the planning committee of the Homiletics and Biblical Studies Section of the Society of Biblical Literature. She is the author of *Transforming Preaching* (Church Publishing, 2010). She has served as a presenter at the annual meeting of the Society of Biblical Literature and a keynote speaker at the Pennsylvania State Pastors' Conference. She received her A.B. degree summa cum laude from Harvard University, where she majored in Comparative Religion. She subsequently earned a masters in performing arts from Emerson College, where she studied the Linklater method of vocal training for actors and became a Designated Linklater Voice Teacher.

She received her master of divinity degree summa cum laude from Yale Divinity School and her Ph.D. in theology from Yale University.

Mark Jefferson, an ordained Baptist minister, is an assistant professor of homiletics at Virginia Theological Seminary. He also serves as associate director of the *Deep Calls to Deep* preaching program, an initiative supported by a Lilly Endowment grant to cultivate embodied preaching. He graduated magna cum laude with a degree in political science from Norfolk State University in 2005 and from the Chandler School of Theology at Emory University in 2008 with a master of divinity. During his time at Candler, he served as president of the Black Student Caucus while pursuing an academic concentration in homiletics and earning a certificate in black church studies. He was awarded the W. E. B. Du Bois *Noomo* Award by the Black Church Studies Program at Candler in 2012. He received his Ph.D. in religion at Emory University in 2019, where his dissertation examined the influence of W. E. B. Du Bois and the idea of the "Talented Tenth" upon the preaching imagination of African American homiletics. He preaches extensively as an invited guest preacher. In 2017, he was inducted into the Martin Luther King, Jr. Board of Preachers at Morehouse College.

Russell J. Levenson Jr. and his wife, Laura, live in Houston, Texas, where he has served as the rector of St. Martin's Episcopal Church since 2007. He received a master of divinity degree from Virginia Theological Seminary in 1992 and accepted the "Dean's Cross" from the seminary in 2012. He completed his doctor of ministry at Beeson Divinity School in 1997 and was awarded Beeson's Distinguished Alumnus Award in 2011. In 2015, he was inducted into the Most Venerable Order of the Hospital of St. John of Jerusalem in 2015. Dr. Levenson has served on the board of advisors for St. Luke's School of Theology and Beeson Divinity School, as well as on the board of the Living Church Foundation, Amazing Place and *Day1*, a national weekly ecumenical radio show. He is the author of several articles in various magazines and religious journals. In 2019 and 2020, he will have a series of four devotional books released by Church Publishing: *Bits of Heaven: A Summer Companion*; *Finding Shelter: An Autumn Companion*; *Preparing Room: An Advent Companion*; and *A Path to Wholeness:*

A Lenten Companion. In addition, he is the author of a new forward for John Claypool's re-released classic work on grief *Tracks of a Fellow Struggler* (Church Publishing).

Ian S. Markham is the dean and president of Virginia Theological Seminary and professor of theology and ethics. He is the author of numerous books, including *An Introduction to Ministry* (co-written with Oran Warder) (Wiley, 2016), *Against Atheism* (Wiley, 2010), *A Theology of Engagement* (Wiley, 2003), *Truth and the Reality of God* (T&T Clark, 1998), and *Plurality and Christian Ethics* (Cambridge University Press, 1994). His awards include the F. D. Maurice Lectures at King's College, London, 2015; Robertson Fellow, 2006; Teape Lecturer in India, 2004; Claggett Fellow attached to Washington National Cathedral in 2000; and Frank Woods Fellow at Trinity College, Melbourne, in 1997.

Phoebe Roaf is bishop of the Diocese of West Tennessee. She formerly served as the rector of St. Philip's Episcopal Church in Richmond, Virginia. When she joined St. Philip's in 2011, she became the first woman to serve as rector of the church in its 150-year history. She was the first African American woman to be ordained as an Episcopal priest in the Diocese of Louisiana. She previously served as associate rector of Trinity New Orleans, the largest Episcopal church in the Diocese of Louisiana, where she was the first person of color to serve as a priest there. She previously served as a member of the Standing Committee, the Resolutions Committee, and the Committee on the Priesthood for the Diocese of Virginia. She holds an undergraduate degree in U.S. history from Harvard College and a master's degree in public affairs from the Woodrow Wilson School at Princeton University. After pursuing a career in public policy, she attended the University of Arkansas at Little Rock School of Law. In the midst of her legal career in New Orleans, she was called to ordained ministry. She received a master of divinity degree from Virginia Theological Seminary in 2008.

Stephanie Spellers is canon to the presiding bishop and primate of the Episcopal Church for Evangelism, Reconciliation, and Stewardship of Creation. She is one of the Episcopal Church's leading thinkers and consultants around twenty-first-century ministry and mission. She is the author of *The Episcopal Way* (the first volume in the new Church's Teachings for a Changing World series) (Morehouse, 2014) and *Radical Welcome: Embracing God, The Other and the Spirit of Transformation* (Church Publishing, 2006). She also teaches and directs programs in mission, reconciliation, and formation at General Theological Seminary in New York City, and serves as a senior consultant for the Center for Progressive Renewal, a nationwide ecumenical consulting and training group. She has served as chaplain to the Episcopal Church's House of Bishops, as co-chair of the Standing Commission on Mission and Evangelism, as chief architect for the legislation that birthed Mission Enterprise Zones, and as founder of the influential emergent ministry The Crossing at St. Paul's Cathedral (www.thecrossingboston. org). She began her career as an award-winning religion journalist in Knoxville, Tennessee, a job she took in 1996 upon graduation from Harvard Divinity School, where she studied religion and movements for social change. She is a contributor to The Work of the People and presented the popular TEDx talk "The Revolutionary Art of Listening" (2016).

Samuel Wells is vicar of St. Martin-in-the-Fields, Trafalgar Square, London. He has been a parish priest for twenty-one years (ten of those in urban priority areas) and was previously dean of Duke University Chapel in North Carolina. In addition, he is visiting professor of Christian ethics at King's College London and is a member of the multi-stakeholder council that advises the G20 meetings. He is a regular contributor to Thought for the Day on BBC Radio 4's *Today* program. He has published thirty-three books, including *Walk Humbly: Encouragements for Living, Working, and Being* (Eerdmans, 2019) and works on Christian ethics, ministry, liturgy, and preaching.